Fun Stuff Cookbook

Publications International, Ltd.

Pictured on the front cover *(clockwise from top left):* Ladybug Cupcakes *(page 114)*, Ice Cream Cake Cones *(page 32)*, Blue's Chillin' Banana Coolers *(page 88)*, and Kids' Favorite Jumbo Chippers *(page 4)*.

Pictured on the back cover *(left to right):* White Chocolate Brownies *(page 24)*, Ultimate Rocky Road Cups *(page 72)*, and Colorful Caramel Apples *(page 112)*.

ISBN-13: 978-1-4508-7364-2
ISBN-10: 1-4508-7364-2

Manufactured in China.

8 7 6 5 4 3 2 1

Microwave Cooking: Microwave ovens vary in wattage. Use the cooking times as guidelines and check for doneness before adding more time.

pi

Publications International, Ltd.

Contents

Colorful Cookies

Kids' Favorite Jumbo Chippers

MAKES 3 DOZEN COOKIES

1	cup (2 sticks) butter, softened
¾	cup granulated sugar
¾	cup packed brown sugar
2	eggs
1	teaspoon vanilla extract
2¼	cups all-purpose flour
1	teaspoon baking soda
¾	teaspoon salt
1¼	cups M&M'S® Milk Chocolate Candies
1	cup peanut butter flavored chips

Preheat oven to 375°F.

In large bowl, cream butter and sugars until light and fluffy; beat in eggs and vanilla. In medium bowl, combine flour, baking soda and salt; blend into creamed mixture. Stir in M&M'S® Chocolate Candies and peanut butter chips. Drop by rounded tablespoonfuls 3 inches apart onto ungreased cookie sheets.

Bake 10 to 12 minutes or until edges are golden brown. Let cookies stand on cookie sheets 2 minutes. Remove cookies to wire racks; cool completely.

Polka Dot Macaroons

MAKES ABOUT 5 DOZEN COOKIES

1 bag (14 ounces) sweetened shredded coconut

1 can (14 ounces) sweetened condensed milk

¾ cup all-purpose flour

1¾ cups M&M'S® Milk Chocolate Candies

Preheat oven to 350°F. Grease cookie sheets; set aside.

In large bowl, combine coconut, condensed milk and flour until well blended. Stir in M&M'S® Milk Chocolate Candies. Drop by rounded tablespoonfuls about 2 inches apart onto prepared cookie sheets.

Bake 8 to 10 minutes or until edges are golden brown. Cool completely on wire racks. Store in tightly covered container.

Red's Ultimate M&M'S® Cookies

MAKES ABOUT 3 DOZEN COOKIES

1 cup (2 sticks) butter, softened

½ cup granulated sugar

½ cup firmly packed light brown sugar

1 large egg

1 teaspoon vanilla extract

2 cups all-purpose flour

½ teaspoon baking soda

⅛ teaspoon salt

2 cups M&M'S® MINIS Milk Chocolate Candies

¾ cup chopped nuts (optional)

Preheat oven to 350°F.

In large bowl, cream butter and sugars until light and fluffy; beat in egg and vanilla. In medium bowl, combine flour, baking soda and salt; blend into creamed mixture. Stir in M&M'S® MINIS Milk Chocolate Candies and nuts, if desired. Drop by heaping tablespoonfuls about 2 inches apart onto ungreased cookie sheets.

Bake 10 to 13 minutes or until edges are lightly browned and centers are still soft. Do not overbake. Cool 1 minute on cookie sheets; cool completely on wire racks. Store in tightly covered container.

Polka Dot Macaroons

Spicy Lemon Crescents

MAKES ABOUT 2 DOZEN COOKIES

1	cup (2 sticks) butter or margarine, softened
1½	cups powdered sugar, divided
½	teaspoon lemon extract
½	teaspoon grated lemon peel
2	cups cake flour
½	cup finely chopped almonds, walnuts or pecans
1	teaspoon ground cinnamon
½	teaspoon ground cardamom
½	teaspoon ground nutmeg
1¾	cups **M&M'S®** Milk Chocolate Candies

Preheat oven to 375°F. Lightly grease cookie sheets; set aside.

In large bowl, cream butter and ½ cup powdered sugar; add lemon extract and peel, beating until well blended. In medium bowl, combine flour, nuts, cinnamon, cardamom and nutmeg; add to creamed mixture until well blended. Stir in **M&M'S®** Milk Chocolate Candies. Using 1 tablespoon of dough at a time, form into crescent shapes; place about 2 inches apart onto prepared cookie sheets.

Bake 12 to 14 minutes or until edges are golden brown. Cool 2 minutes on cookie sheets. Gently roll warm crescents in remaining 1 cup powdered sugar. Cool completely on wire racks. Store in tightly covered container.

Tasty Tidbit

These shortbread cookies are a holiday (and everyday) favorite.

Chocolate Raspberry Thumbprints

MAKES ABOUT 4 DOZEN COOKIES

½   **cup (1 stick) butter or margarine, softened**

½   **cup granulated sugar**

½   **cup firmly packed light brown sugar**

1   **large egg**

1   **egg white**

1   **teaspoon vanilla extract**

2   **cups all-purpose flour**

½   **teaspoon baking powder**

1¾   **cups M&M'S® MINIS Milk Chocolate Candies, divided**

   Powdered sugar

½   **cup raspberry jam**

Melt butter in microwave in large microwave-safe bowl; add sugars and mix well. Stir in egg, egg white and vanilla.

In medium bowl, combine flour and baking powder; blend into butter mixture. Stir in 1¼ cups **M&M'S® MINIS** Milk Chocolate Candies; refrigerate dough 1 hour.

Preheat oven to 350°F. Lightly grease cookie sheets. Roll dough into 1-inch balls and place about 2 inches apart onto prepared cookie sheets. Make an indentation in center of each ball with thumb.

Bake 8 to 10 minutes. Remove from oven and re-indent, if necessary; transfer to wire racks.

Lightly dust warm cookies with powdered sugar; fill each indentation with ½ teaspoon raspberry jam. Sprinkle with remaining ½ cup **M&M'S® MINIS** Milk Chocolate Candies. Cool completely. Dust with additional powdered sugar, if desired. Store in tightly covered container.

Tasty Tidbit

A favorite anytime of the year, these bite-sized cookies are sure to please little (and big) appetites.

Crispy Oat Drops

MAKES ABOUT 4 DOZEN COOKIES

1	cup (2 sticks) butter or margarine, softened
½	cup granulated sugar
½	cup firmly packed light brown sugar
1	large egg
2	cups all-purpose flour
½	cup quick-cooking or old-fashioned oats, uncooked
1	teaspoon cream of tartar
½	teaspoon baking soda
¼	teaspoon salt
1¾	cups **M&M'S®** Milk Chocolate Candies
1	cup toasted rice cereal
½	cup sweetened shredded coconut
½	cup coarsely chopped pecans

Preheat oven to 350°F.

In large bowl, cream butter and sugars until light and fluffy; beat in egg. In medium bowl, combine flour, oats, cream of tartar, baking soda and salt; blend flour mixture into creamed mixture. Stir in **M&M'S®** Milk Chocolate Candies, cereal, coconut and pecans. Drop by heaping tablespoonfuls about 2 inches apart onto ungreased cookie sheets.

Bake 10 to 13 minutes or until lightly browned. Cool completely on wire racks. Store in tightly covered container.

Tasty Tidbit

Crispy and crunchy—a great combination of flavors perfect for an afternoon snack.

Tic-Tac-Toe Cookies

MAKES 4 DOZEN COOKIES

¾ cup (1½ sticks) butter, softened

¾ cup granulated sugar

1 large egg

1 teaspoon vanilla extract

2¼ cups all-purpose flour

½ teaspoon baking powder

¼ teaspoon salt

4 squares (1 ounce each) semi-sweet chocolate, melted

¼ cup powdered sugar

1 teaspoon water

½ cup M&M'S® MINIS Milk Chocolate Candies

In large bowl, cream butter and granulated sugar until light and fluffy; beat in egg and vanilla. In small bowl, combine flour, baking powder and salt; blend into creamed mixture. Reserve half of dough. Stir chocolate into remaining dough. Wrap and refrigerate doughs 30 minutes.

Working with one dough at a time on lightly floured surface, roll or pat into 7×4½-inch rectangle. Cut dough into 9 (7×½-inch) strips. Repeat with remaining dough. Place one strip chocolate dough on sheet of plastic wrap.

Place one strip vanilla dough next to chocolate dough. Place second strip of chocolate dough next to vanilla dough to make bottom layer. Prepare second row by stacking strips on first row, alternating vanilla dough over chocolate, and chocolate dough over vanilla. Repeat with third row to complete 1 bar. Repeat entire process with remaining dough strips, starting with vanilla dough, to complete second bar. Wrap both bars and refrigerate 1 hour.

Preheat oven to 350°F. Lightly grease cookie sheets. Cut bars crosswise into ¼-inch slices. Place 2 inches apart on prepared cookie sheets. Bake 10 to 12 minutes. Cool on cookie sheets 2 minutes; cool completely on wire racks.

In small bowl, combine powdered sugar and water until smooth. Using icing to attach, decorate cookies with **M&M'S® MINIS** Milk Chocolate Candies to look like Tic-Tac-Toe games. Store in tightly covered container.

Chocolate Cherry Treats

MAKES 3 DOZEN COOKIES

- ½ cup (1 stick) butter, softened
- ¾ cup firmly packed light brown sugar
- ¼ cup granulated sugar
- ½ cup sour cream
- 1 large egg
- 1 tablespoon maraschino cherry juice
- 1 teaspoon vanilla extract
- 2 cups all-purpose flour
- ½ teaspoon baking soda
- ¼ teaspoon salt
- 1¼ cups M&M'S® MINIS Milk Chocolate Candies
- ½ cup chopped walnuts
- ⅓ cup well-drained chopped maraschino cherries

Preheat oven to 350°F.

In large bowl, cream butter and sugars until light and fluffy; beat in sour cream, egg, maraschino cherry juice and vanilla. In medium bowl, combine flour, baking soda and salt; add to creamed mixture. Stir in M&M'S® MINIS Milk Chocolate Candies, walnuts and maraschino cherries. Drop by heaping tablespoonfuls about 2 inches apart onto ungreased cookie sheets.

Bake about 15 minutes. Cool 1 minute on cookie sheets; cool completely on wire racks. Store in tightly covered container.

Colorful Cookie Buttons

MAKES 3 DOZEN COOKIES

1½	cups (3 sticks) butter, softened
½	cup granulated sugar
½	cup firmly packed light brown sugar
2	large egg yolks
1	teaspoon vanilla extract
3½	cups all-purpose flour
1½	teaspoons baking powder
½	teaspoon salt
1	cup M&M'S® MINIS Milk Chocolate Candies

Preheat oven to 350°F.

In large bowl, cream butter and sugars until light and fluffy; beat in egg yolks and vanilla. In medium bowl, combine flour, baking powder and salt; add to creamed mixture.

Shape dough into 72 balls. For each cookie, place one ball on ungreased cookie sheet and flatten. Place 8 to 10 M&M'S® MINIS Milk Chocolate Candies on dough. Flatten second ball and place over M&M'S® MINIS Milk Chocolate Candies, pressing top and bottom dough together. Decorate top with remaining M&M'S® MINIS Milk Chocolate Candies. Repeat with remaining dough balls and M&M'S® MINIS Milk Chocolate Candies, placing cookies about 2 inches apart on cookie sheets.

Bake 17 to 18 minutes. Cool 2 minutes on cookie sheets; cool completely on wire racks. Store in tightly covered container.

Brownie Turtle Cookies

MAKES ABOUT 2½ DOZEN COOKIES

- 2 squares (1 ounce each) unsweetened baking chocolate
- ⅓ cup solid vegetable shortening
- 1 cup granulated sugar
- 2 large eggs
- ½ teaspoon vanilla extract
- 1¼ cups all-purpose flour
- ½ teaspoon baking powder
- ½ teaspoon salt
- 1 cup M&M'S® MINIS Milk Chocolate Candies, divided
- 1 cup pecan halves
- ⅓ cup caramel ice cream topping
- ⅓ cup sweetened shredded coconut
- ⅓ cup finely chopped pecans

Preheat oven to 350°F. Lightly grease cookie sheets; set aside.

Heat chocolate and shortening in 2-quart saucepan over low heat, stirring constantly until melted; remove from heat. Mix in sugar, eggs and vanilla. Blend in flour, baking powder and salt. Stir in ⅔ cup M&M'S® MINIS Milk Chocolate Candies.

For each cookie, arrange 3 pecan halves, with ends almost touching at center, on prepared cookie sheets. Drop dough by rounded teaspoonfuls onto center of each group of pecans; mound the dough slightly. Bake 8 to 10 minutes or just until set. Do not overbake. Cool completely on wire racks.

In small bowl, combine ice cream topping, coconut and chopped nuts; top each cookie with about 1½ teaspoons mixture. Press remaining ⅓ cup M&M'S® MINIS Milk Chocolate Candies into topping.

Orange Coconut Cream Bars

MAKES 24 BARS

1 package (18.25 ounces) yellow cake mix

1 cup quick-cooking or old-fashioned oats, uncooked

¾ cup chopped nuts

½ cup (1 stick) butter or margarine, melted

1 large egg

1 can (14 ounces) sweetened condensed milk

2 teaspoons grated orange peel

1 cup sweetened shredded coconut

1 cup M&M'S® Milk Chocolate Candies

Preheat oven to 375°F. Lightly grease 13×9×2-inch baking pan; set aside.

In large bowl, combine cake mix, oats, nuts, butter and egg until ingredients are thoroughly moistened and mixture resembles coarse crumbs. Reserve 1 cup mixture. Firmly press remaining mixture onto bottom of prepared pan; bake 10 minutes.

In separate bowl, combine condensed milk and orange peel; spread over baked base. Combine reserved crumb mixture, coconut and M&M'S® Milk Chocolate Candies; sprinkle evenly over condensed milk mixture and press in lightly. Continue baking 20 to 25 minutes or until golden brown. Cool completely. Cut into bars. Store in tightly covered container.

Chocolate Orange Gems

MAKES 24 BARS

⅔ cup butter-flavored solid vegetable shortening

¾ cup firmly packed light brown sugar

1 large egg

¼ cup orange juice

1 tablespoon grated orange peel

2¼ cups all-purpose flour

½ teaspoon baking powder

½ teaspoon baking soda

½ teaspoon salt

1¾ cups M&M'S® Milk Chocolate Candies

1 cup coarsely chopped pecans

⅓ cup orange marmalade

Vanilla Glaze (recipe follows)

Preheat oven to 350°F.

In large bowl, cream shortening and brown sugar until light and fluffy; beat in egg, orange juice and orange peel. In medium bowl, combine flour, baking powder, baking soda and salt; blend into creamed mixture. Stir in M&M'S® Milk Chocolate Candies and nuts. Reserve 1 cup dough; spread remaining dough in ungreased 13×9×2-inch baking pan.

Spread marmalade evenly over top of dough to within ½ inch of edges. Drop reserved dough by teaspoonfuls randomly over marmalade.

Bake 25 to 30 minutes or until light golden brown. Do not overbake. Cool completely; drizzle with Vanilla Glaze. Cut into bars. Store in tightly covered container.

Vanilla Glaze: Combine 1 cup powdered sugar and 1 to 1½ tablespoons warm water until desired consistency. Place glaze in resealable plastic sandwich bag; seal bag. Cut a tiny piece off one corner of the bag (not more than ⅛ inch).

Tasty Tidbit

A touch of orange adds an extra tang of flavor to these tasty bars.

Double-Decker Confetti Brownies

MAKES 24 BROWNIES

¾ cup (1½ sticks) butter or margarine, softened

1 cup granulated sugar

1 cup firmly packed light brown sugar

3 eggs

1 teaspoon vanilla extract

2½ cups all-purpose flour, divided

2½ teaspoons baking powder

½ teaspoon salt

⅓ cup unsweetened cocoa powder

2 tablespoons butter or margarine, melted

1 cup M&M'S® Milk Chocolate Candies, divided

Preheat oven to 350°F. Lightly grease 13×9×2-inch baking pan; set aside.

In large bowl, cream ¾ cup butter and sugars until light and fluffy; beat in eggs and vanilla. In medium bowl, combine 2¼ cups flour, baking powder and salt; blend into creamed mixture. Divide batter in half. Blend together cocoa powder and melted butter; stir into one half of the dough. Spread cocoa dough evenly into prepared baking pan.

Stir remaining ¼ cup flour and ½ cup M&M'S® Milk Chocolate Candies into remaining dough; spread evenly over cocoa dough in pan. Sprinkle with remaining ½ cup M&M'S® Milk Chocolate Candies. Bake 25 to 30 minutes or until edges start to pull away from sides of pan. Cool completely. Cut into bars. Store in tightly covered container.

Tasty Tidbit

These brownies can be cut into traditional squares or into triangles for a unique presentation.

White Chocolate Brownies

MAKES 16 BROWNIES

6   tablespoons butter

5   squares (1 ounce each) white chocolate, divided

1   large egg

½   cup granulated sugar

¾   cup all-purpose flour

¾   teaspoon vanilla extract

¼   teaspoon salt

1¼   cups M&M'S® Milk Chocolate Candies, divided

½   cup chopped walnuts

Preheat oven to 325°F. Lightly grease 8×8×2-inch baking pan; set aside.

In small saucepan, melt butter and 4 squares white chocolate over low heat; stir to blend. Remove from heat; let cool slightly. In medium bowl, beat egg and sugar until light; stir in white chocolate mixture, flour, vanilla and salt. Spread batter evenly in prepared pan. Sprinkle with ¾ cup M&M'S® Milk Chocolate Candies and walnuts.

Bake 35 to 37 minutes or until firm in center. Cool completely on wire rack.

Place remaining 1 square white chocolate in small microwave-safe bowl. Microwave on HIGH 20 seconds; stir. Repeat as necessary until white chocolate is completely melted, stirring at 10-second intervals. Drizzle over brownies and sprinkle with remaining ½ cup M&M'S® Milk Chocolate Candies. Cut into bars. Store in tightly covered container.

Tasty Tidbit ©

Two kinds of chocolate make these brownies doubly-delicious.

Chocolate Marbled Blondies

MAKES 16 BARS

½ cup (1 stick) butter or margarine, softened

½ cup firmly packed light brown sugar

1 large egg

2 teaspoons vanilla extract

1½ cups all-purpose flour

1¼ teaspoons baking soda

1 cup **M&M'S®** Milk Chocolate Candies, divided

4 ounces cream cheese, softened

2 tablespoons granulated sugar

1 large egg yolk

¼ cup unsweetened cocoa powder

Preheat oven to 350°F. Lightly grease 9×9×2-inch baking pan; set aside.

In large bowl, cream butter and brown sugar until light and fluffy; beat in egg and vanilla. In medium bowl, combine flour and baking soda; blend into creamed mixture. Stir in ⅔ cup **M&M'S®** Milk Chocolate Candies; set aside. Dough will be stiff. In separate bowl, beat together cream cheese, granulated sugar and egg yolk until smooth; stir in cocoa powder until well blended.

Place chocolate-cheese mixture in 6 equal portions evenly onto bottom of prepared pan. Place reserved dough around cheese mixture and swirl slightly with tines of fork. Pat down evenly on top. Sprinkle with remaining ⅓ cup **M&M'S®** Milk Chocolate Candies.

Bake 25 to 30 minutes or until toothpick inserted in center comes out with moist crumbs. Cool completely. Cut into bars. Store in refrigerator in tightly covered container.

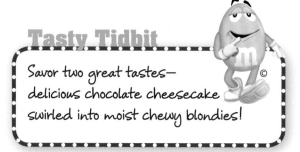

Tasty Tidbit

Savor two great tastes— delicious chocolate cheesecake swirled into moist chewy blondies!

Cranberry Cheese Bars

MAKES 32 BARS

2 cups all-purpose flour

1½ cups quick-cooking or old-fashioned oats, uncooked

¾ cup plus 1 tablespoon firmly packed light brown sugar, divided

1 cup (2 sticks) butter or margarine, softened

1¾ cups **M&M'S®** Milk Chocolate Candies, divided

1 package (8 ounces) cream cheese

1 can (14 ounces) sweetened condensed milk

¼ cup lemon juice

1 teaspoon vanilla extract

2 tablespoons cornstarch

1 can (16 ounces) whole berry cranberry sauce

Preheat oven to 350°F. Lightly grease 13×9×2-inch baking pan; set aside.

In large bowl, combine flour, oats, ¾ cup brown sugar and butter; mix until crumbly. Reserve 1½ cups crumb mixture for topping. Stir ½ cup **M&M'S®** Milk Chocolate Candies into remaining crumb mixture; press into prepared pan. Bake 15 minutes. Cool completely.

In large bowl, beat cream cheese until light and fluffy; gradually mix in condensed milk, lemon juice and vanilla until smooth. Pour evenly over crust.

In small bowl, combine remaining 1 tablespoon brown sugar, cornstarch and cranberry sauce. Spoon over cream cheese mixture. Stir remaining 1¼ cups **M&M'S®** Milk Chocolate Candies into reserved crumb mixture. Sprinkle over cranberry mixture. Bake 40 minutes. Cool at room temperature; refrigerate before cutting. Store in refrigerator in tightly covered container.

Tasty Tidbit

No need to wait for a special occasion to enjoy these chocolatey, fruity cheesecake bars!

Yellow's Nuts for Nutty Squares

MAKES 24 BARS

1   cup (2 sticks) plus 2 tablespoons butter, softened and divided

½   cup powdered sugar

2¼ cups all-purpose flour

¼   teaspoon salt

¾   cup granulated sugar

½   cup light corn syrup

2   large eggs, beaten

½   teaspoon vanilla extract

2   cups coarsely chopped mixed nuts

1   cup M&M'S® MINIS Milk Chocolate Candies

Preheat oven to 325°F. Lightly grease 13×9-inch baking pan; set aside.

In large bowl, cream 1 cup (2 sticks) butter and powdered sugar until light and fluffy; gradually add flour and salt until well blended. Press dough evenly onto bottom and ½ inch up sides of prepared pan. Bake 25 to 30 minutes or until very light golden brown.

In small saucepan, melt remaining 2 tablespoons butter; let cool slightly. In large bowl, combine melted butter, granulated sugar, corn syrup, eggs and vanilla. Pour filling over partially baked crust; sprinkle with nuts and M&M'S® MINIS Milk Chocolate Candies. Return to oven; bake 30 to 35 minutes or until filling is set. Remove pan to wire rack; cool completely. Cut into bars. Store in tightly covered container.

Almond Brownies

MAKES 16 BROWNIES

½ cup (1 stick) butter

2 squares (1 ounce each) unsweetened baking chocolate

2 large eggs

1 cup firmly packed light brown sugar

¼ teaspoon almond extract

½ cup all-purpose flour

1½ cups M&M'S® MINIS Milk Chocolate Candies, divided

½ cup slivered almonds, toasted and divided

Chocolate Glaze (recipe follows)

Preheat oven to 350°F. Grease and flour 8×8×2-inch baking pan; set aside.

In small saucepan, melt butter and chocolate over low heat; stir to blend. Remove from heat; let cool. In medium bowl, beat eggs and brown sugar until well blended; stir in chocolate mixture and almond extract. Add flour. Stir in 1 cup M&M'S® MINIS Milk Chocolate Candies and ¼ cup almonds. Spread batter evenly in prepared pan.

Bake 25 to 28 minutes or until firm in center. Cool completely on wire rack.

Prepare Chocolate Glaze. Spread over brownies; decorate with remaining ½ cup M&M'S® MINIS Milk Chocolate Candies and remaining ¼ cup almonds. Cut into bars. Store in tightly covered container.

Chocolate Glaze: In small saucepan over low heat, combine 4 teaspoons water and 1 tablespoon butter; heat to boiling. Stir in 4 teaspoons unsweetened cocoa powder. Gradually stir in ½ cup powdered sugar until smooth. Remove from heat; stir in ¼ teaspoon vanilla. Cool slightly before spreading over brownies.

Ice Cream Cake Cones

MAKES 2 DOZEN CAKE CONES

1	cup all-purpose flour
2	teaspoons baking powder
¼	teaspoon salt
¾	cup granulated sugar
¼	cup (½ stick) butter, softened
½	cup milk
½	teaspoon vanilla extract
2	large eggs
24	flat-bottomed ice cream cones
1¼	cups M&M'S® MINIS Milk Chocolate Candies, divided
1	cup thawed frozen nondairy whipped topping
1	cup any flavor frosting

Preheat oven to 350°F.

In large bowl, combine flour, baking powder and salt; stir in sugar. Beat in butter, milk and vanilla. Beat 2 minutes. Add eggs; beat 2 minutes. Stand 24 ice cream cones on 2 cookie sheets. Divide batter evenly among cones. Sprinkle evenly with ¾ cup M&M'S® MINIS Milk Chocolate Candies.

Bake 20 to 25 minutes or until toothpick inserted in center comes out clean. Cool completely on wire racks.

In small bowl, combine whipped topping and frosting. Frost cupcakes with frosting mixture, mounding to look like ice cream. Decorate with remaining ½ cup M&M'S® MINIS Milk Chocolate Candies. Serve immediately.

Colorful Streusel Coffeecake

MAKES 12 SLICES

¾ cup (1½ sticks) butter or margarine, divided

1 cup granulated sugar

2 large eggs

1 teaspoon vanilla extract

2½ cups all-purpose flour, divided

1 teaspoon baking powder

1¾ cups M&M'S® Milk Chocolate Candies, divided

4 TWIX® Candy Bars, chopped

½ cup firmly packed light brown sugar

Preheat oven to 350°F. Grease 9-inch springform pan.

In large bowl, cream ½ cup butter and granulated sugar until light and fluffy; beat in eggs and vanilla. In medium bowl, combine 2 cups flour and baking powder; blend into creamed mixture. Do not overmix. Stir in ¾ cup M&M'S® Milk Chocolate Candies. Spread batter into prepared pan.

In separate bowl, combine chopped TWIX® Candy Bars, remaining ½ cup flour, brown sugar and ¼ cup melted butter to create streusel. Add remaining 1 cup M&M'S® Milk Chocolate Candies and toss to mix. Sprinkle streusel evenly over batter.

Bake 35 to 40 minutes or until golden and firm to the touch. Cool completely before removing side of pan. Store in tightly covered container.

Tasty Tidbit

Make your next coffee break or brunch more festive with this tasty cake.

Fudgy Ripple Cake

MAKES 10 SERVINGS

1   package (18.25 ounces) yellow cake mix, plus ingredients to prepare mix

1   package (3 ounces) cream cheese, softened

2   tablespoons unsweetened cocoa powder

      Fudgy Glaze (recipe follows)

½   cup M&M'S® MINIS Milk Chocolate Candies

Preheat oven to 350°F. Lightly grease and flour 10-inch bundt or ring pan; set aside.

Prepare cake mix as package directs. In medium bowl, combine 1½ cups prepared batter, cream cheese and cocoa powder until smooth. Pour half of yellow batter into prepared pan. Drop spoonfuls of chocolate batter over yellow batter in pan. Top with remaining yellow batter. Bake about 45 minutes or until toothpick inserted near center comes out clean. Cool completely on wire rack.

Unmold cake onto serving plate. Prepare Fudgy Glaze; spread over top of cake, allowing some glaze to run over side. Sprinkle with M&M'S® MINIS Milk Chocolate Candies. Store in tightly covered container.

Fudgy Glaze

1   square (1 ounce) semi-sweet chocolate

1   cup powdered sugar

⅓   cup unsweetened cocoa powder

3   tablespoons milk

½   teaspoon vanilla extract

Place chocolate in small microwave-safe bowl. Microwave on HIGH 30 seconds; stir. Repeat as necessary until chocolate is completely melted, stirring at 10-second intervals; set aside.

In medium bowl, combine powdered sugar and cocoa powder. Stir in milk, vanilla and melted chocolate until smooth.

Tasty Tidbit

This moist cake is a real crowd-pleaser.

Grasshopper Cheesecake

MAKES 8 SERVINGS

- 2 cups dark chocolate sandwich cookie crumbs
- ⅔ cup **M&M'S® MINIS** Milk Chocolate Candies, divided
- 2½ tablespoons butter, melted
- 11 ounces cream cheese, softened
- ⅔ cup granulated sugar
- 1 to 1¼ teaspoons mint extract
- 1 teaspoon vanilla extract
- 3 to 4 drops green food coloring
- 1 cup thawed frozen nondairy whipped topping
- ⅓ cup hot fudge ice cream topping, warmed

Preheat oven to 325°F.

In medium bowl, combine cookie crumbs, ⅓ cup **M&M'S® MINIS** Milk Chocolate Candies and butter. Press onto bottom and up side of 9-inch pie plate. Bake 10 minutes. Cool completely on wire rack.

In large bowl, beat cream cheese and sugar until light and fluffy; add mint extract, vanilla and food coloring. Stir in whipped topping. Spread cream cheese mixture in prepared crust. Cover and freeze until firm and ready to serve.

Just before serving, drizzle pie with hot fudge topping. Sprinkle with remaining ⅓ cup **M&M'S® MINIS** Milk Chocolate Candies. Garnish with additional whipped topping. Store covered in freezer.

Tasty Tidbit

Cool mint and deep dark chocolate make this sensational dessert irresistible.

Nothin' But Love Brownie Cake

MAKES 10 SERVINGS

½ cup (1 stick) butter, softened

1⅔ cups granulated sugar

1 large egg

¾ teaspoon vanilla extract

1⅓ cups all-purpose flour

⅔ cup unsweetened cocoa powder

1 teaspoon baking soda

⅛ teaspoon salt

⅔ cup sour cream

¼ cup buttermilk

1½ cups M&M'S® Milk Chocolate Candies, divided

1 container (16 ounces) white frosting

Preheat oven to 350°F. Lightly grease bottoms of 1 (8-inch) round cake pan and 1 (8×8×2-inch) baking pan. Line pans with waxed paper; lightly grease and flour pans; set aside.

In large bowl, cream butter and sugar until light and fluffy; beat in egg and vanilla. In medium bowl, combine flour, cocoa powder, baking soda and salt. In small bowl, combine sour cream and buttermilk; add to creamed mixture alternately with dry ingredients, beginning and ending with flour mixture. Divide batter evenly between prepared pans. Sprinkle batter in each pan with ½ cup M&M'S® Milk Chocolate Candies.

Bake about 35 minutes or until toothpick inserted in center comes out clean. Cool completely on wire racks.

Cut round cake in half to make two semi-circles. Place square cake layer on large serving plate. Position one semi-circle cake along one side of square cake, connecting with some frosting. Position remaining semi-circle cake along adjacent side of square cake, to make heart shape; connect with some frosting. Frost entire cake with remaining frosting. Decorate with remaining ½ cup M&M'S® Milk Chocolate Candies. Store in tightly covered container.

Tasty Tidbit

Show your valentine how much you care.

Strawberry Cheesecake Squares

MAKES 16 BARS

2	large eggs, divided
1	cup M&M'S® MINIS Milk Chocolate Candies, divided
¾	cup graham cracker crumbs
⅓	cup plus 2 tablespoons granulated sugar, divided
2	tablespoons butter, melted
1	package (8 ounces) cream cheese, softened
1	teaspoon vanilla extract
½	cup seedless strawberry jam
	Powdered sugar

Preheat oven to 350°F. Lightly grease 8×8×2-inch baking pan; set aside.

In small bowl, separate 1 egg white, reserving egg yolk in another small bowl. In medium bowl, combine ⅓ cup M&M'S® MINIS Milk Chocolate Candies, cracker crumbs and 2 tablespoons granulated sugar; stir in butter and 1 egg white. Press dough evenly onto bottom of prepared pan. Bake 8 minutes; cool 5 minutes on wire rack.

In large bowl, beat cream cheese and remaining ⅓ cup granulated sugar; add reserved egg yolk, remaining whole egg and vanilla until well blended.

In small bowl, stir jam until smooth. Spread jam evenly over crust. Spread cream cheese mixture evenly over jam layer. Bake 20 minutes. Sprinkle with ⅓ cup M&M'S® MINIS Milk Chocolate Candies; press down slightly. Bake 10 to 15 minutes more or until filling is set. Cool completely on wire rack.

Sprinkle with powdered sugar and remaining ⅓ cup M&M'S® MINIS Milk Chocolate Candies. Cut into squares. Store in tightly covered container in refrigerator.

Tasty Tidbit

Any day is a special day when you serve these delicate bars.

Red's Rockin' Rainbow Cupcakes

MAKES 24 CUPCAKES

2¼ cups all-purpose flour

1 tablespoon baking powder

½ teaspoon salt

1⅔ cups granulated sugar

½ cup (1 stick) butter, softened

1 cup milk

2 teaspoons vanilla extract

3 large egg whites

Blue and assorted food colorings

1½ cups M&M'S® MINIS Milk Chocolate Candies, divided

1 container (16 ounces) white frosting

Preheat oven to 350°F. Lightly grease 24 (2¾-inch) muffin cups or line with paper or foil liners; set aside.

In large bowl, combine flour, baking powder and salt. Blend in sugar, butter, milk and vanilla; beat about 2 minutes. Add egg whites; beat 2 minutes. Divide batter evenly among prepared muffin cups. Place 2 drops desired food coloring into each muffin cup. Swirl gently with knife. Sprinkle evenly with ¾ cup M&M'S® MINIS Milk Chocolate Candies.

Bake 20 to 25 minutes or until toothpick inserted in center comes out clean. Cool completely on wire racks.

Combine frosting and blue food coloring. Spread frosting over cupcakes; decorate with remaining ¾ cup M&M'S® MINIS Milk Chocolate Candies to make rainbows. Store in tightly covered container.

Peppermint Swirl Cake

MAKES 16 SERVINGS

1	package (16 ounces) angel food cake mix
1¼	cups water
4	cups powdered sugar, divided
1	package (8 ounces) cream cheese, softened
½	teaspoon peppermint extract
½	teaspoon vanilla extract
3	to 4 drops red food coloring
2	cups thawed frozen nondairy whipped topping
1¼	cups **M&M'S®** Milk Chocolate Candies, divided
	Additional powdered sugar and nondairy whipped topping for garnish

Preheat oven to 350°F. Line 2 (15×10×1-inch) jelly-roll pans with parchment paper.

Prepare cake mix as package directs using water. Spread half of batter in each prepared pan; bake about 15 minutes or until toothpick inserted in center comes out clean. Cool 10 minutes.

Sprinkle 2 towels with ¼ cup powdered sugar each. Loosen cake edges and turn out onto prepared towels. Carefully peel off parchment paper. Roll up cakes with towels inside, starting at narrow ends; cool completely.

In large bowl, beat cream cheese, 3½ cups powdered sugar, peppermint extract, vanilla and food coloring. Stir in whipped topping. Unroll cakes and spread with peppermint filling. Sprinkle each cake with ½ cup **M&M'S®** Milk Chocolate Candies. Re-roll cakes; sprinkle with powdered sugar.

Decorate each cake with additional whipped topping and remaining ¼ cup **M&M'S®** Milk Chocolate Candies. Store covered in refrigerator.

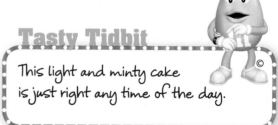

Tasty Tidbit

This light and minty cake is just right any time of the day.

Jeweled Brownie Cheesecake

MAKES 12 SLICES

¾ cup (1½ sticks) butter or margarine

4 squares (1 ounce each) unsweetened baking chocolate

1½ cups plus 2 tablespoons granulated sugar, divided

4 large eggs

1 cup all-purpose flour

1¾ cups **M&M'S® MINIS** Milk Chocolate Candies, divided

½ cup chopped walnuts (optional)

1 package (8 ounces) cream cheese, softened

1 teaspoon vanilla extract

Preheat oven to 350°F. Lightly grease 9-inch springform pan; set aside.

Place butter and chocolate in large microwave-safe bowl. Microwave on HIGH 1 minute; stir. Microwave on HIGH an additional 30 seconds; stir until chocolate is completely melted. Add 1½ cups sugar and 3 eggs, one at a time, beating well after each addition; blend in flour. Stir in 1¼ cups **M&M'S® MINIS** Milk Chocolate Candies and nuts, if desired; set aside.

In large bowl, beat cream cheese and remaining sugar. Add remaining 1 egg and vanilla. Spread half of the chocolate mixture in prepared pan. Carefully spread cream cheese mixture evenly over chocolate mixture, leaving 1-inch border. Spread remaining chocolate mixture evenly over top, all the way to the edges. Sprinkle with remaining ½ cup **M&M'S® MINIS** Milk Chocolate Candies.

Bake 40 to 45 minutes or until firm to the touch. Cool completely. Store in refrigerator in tightly covered container.

"Go Fly a Kite" Cupcakes

MAKES 24 CUPCAKES

1⅔	cups all-purpose flour
½	cup unsweetened cocoa powder
1	teaspoon baking powder
½	teaspoon baking soda
¼	teaspoon salt
1¾	cups granulated sugar
¼	cup firmly packed light brown sugar
½	cup vegetable shortening
1	cup buttermilk
3	large eggs
2	tablespoons vegetable oil
¾	teaspoon vanilla extract
1½	cups **M&M'S® MINIS** Milk Chocolate Candies, divided
24	graham cracker squares
1	container (16 ounces) white frosting
	Assorted food colorings

Preheat oven to 350°F. Lightly grease 24 (2¾-inch) muffin cups or line with foil or paper liners; set aside.

In large bowl, combine flour, cocoa powder, baking powder, baking soda and salt; stir in sugars. Beat in shortening until well combined. Beat in buttermilk, eggs, oil and vanilla. Divide batter among prepared muffin cups. Sprinkle 1 teaspoon **M&M'S® MINIS** Milk Chocolate Candies over batter in each muffin cup.

Bake 20 to 25 minutes or until toothpick inserted in center comes out clean. Cool completely on wire racks.

Using serrated knife and back and forth sawing motion, gently cut graham crackers into kite shapes. (Do not press down on cracker while cutting.) Reserve 1 cup frosting. Tint remaining frosting desired color. Frost graham crackers and decorate with **M&M'S® MINIS** Milk Chocolate Candies. Tint reserved frosting sky blue; frost cupcakes. Place small blob frosting at one edge of cupcake; stand kites in frosting on cupcakes. Make kite tails with **M&M'S® MINIS** Milk Chocolate Candies. Store in tightly covered container.

Blue's Best Banana Bread Pudding

MAKES 8 TO 10 SERVINGS

4	large eggs, beaten
½	cup granulated sugar
¼	cup firmly packed light brown sugar
3	cups milk
1½	tablespoons vanilla extract
1	teaspoon ground cinnamon
8	slices bread, crusts removed
¼	cup (½ stick) butter, softened
1	large ripe banana, sliced
¾	cup M&M'S® Milk Chocolate Candies, divided
1¼	cups caramel ice cream topping, warmed

Lightly grease 8×8×2-inch baking pan; set aside.

In large bowl, combine eggs, sugars, milk, vanilla and cinnamon; set aside. Spread both sides of each bread slice with butter. Layer half of bread slices in prepared pan. Layer banana slices over bread. Layer with remaining bread slices. Pour egg mixture over bread; let stand 15 minutes.

Preheat oven to 350°F. Sprinkle pudding with ¼ cup **M&M'S®** Milk Chocolate Candies. Bake 50 to 55 minutes. Serve warm with caramel topping and remaining ½ cup M&M'S® Milk Chocolate Candies. Store covered in refrigerator.

Apple-Cranberry Turnovers

MAKES 10 SERVINGS

3	cups water
1	teaspoon lemon juice
1	medium apple, peeled and cored
4½	teaspoons granulated sugar, divided
½	teaspoon ground cinnamon
10	sheets frozen phyllo dough, thawed
¾	cup (1½ sticks) butter, melted
¼	cup sweetened dried cranberries
¾	cup M&M'S® MINIS Milk Chocolate Candies
	White Glaze (recipe follows)

In medium bowl, combine water and lemon juice. Cut apple into ½-inch chunks; place apple pieces in lemon water.

In small bowl, combine 2 teaspoons sugar and cinnamon. Place 1 sheet phyllo dough at a time on flat surface and brush immediately with melted butter.* Fold sheet in half lengthwise. Brush with butter again; fold in half lengthwise again. Place about 1 tablespoon apple pieces, about 1 teaspoon cranberries and 1 teaspoon M&M'S® MINIS Milk Chocolate Candies on 1 end of phyllo strip; sprinkle with ¼ teaspoon cinnamon-sugar. Fold over 1 corner to make triangle. Continue folding end to end, as if folding a flag, keeping edges straight. Brush top with butter; sprinkle with ¼ teaspoon sugar. Repeat process with all remaining ingredients.

Place triangles in single layer, seam-side down, on ungreased baking sheet.

Bake at 400°F 8 to 10 minutes or until lightly browned. Cool on pan 1 minute. Remove to wire racks; cool completely.

Prepare White Glaze. Drizzle glaze over turnovers; sprinkle with remaining M&M'S® MINIS Milk Chocolate Candies. Store in tightly covered container.

Keep remaining phyllo sheets covered with large sheet of plastic wrap and damp, clean kitchen towel to keep from drying out.

White Glaze: In small bowl, combine ⅓ cup powdered sugar and 1 tablespoon milk. If necessary, add additional milk, 1 teaspoon at a time, to make pourable glaze.

Chewy Chocolate Granola Treats

MAKES 48 BARS

¼ cup (½ stick) butter or margarine, softened

¼ cup solid vegetable shortening

1 cup firmly packed light brown sugar

1 large egg

1½ teaspoons vanilla extract

1 cup all-purpose flour

½ teaspoon baking soda

¼ teaspoon salt

½ teaspoon ground cinnamon

¼ cup milk

2 cups granola cereal

1¾ cups **M&M'S®** Milk Chocolate Candies, divided

1 cup sweetened shredded coconut

Preheat oven to 350°F. Grease 15×10×1-inch baking pan; set aside.

In large bowl, cream butter, shortening, brown sugar, egg and vanilla. In medium bowl, combine flour, baking soda, salt and cinnamon; blend into creamed mixture alternately with milk. Stir in cereal, 1¼ cups **M&M'S®** Milk Chocolate Candies and coconut. Spread mixture into prepared pan; sprinkle with remaining ½ cup **M&M'S®** Milk Chocolate Candies and press in lightly.

Bake 25 to 30 minutes until golden. Cool completely. Cut into bars. Store in tightly covered container.

Tasty Tidbit

Treat yourself to these crunchy, chewy delights.

Marbled Biscotti

MAKES 24 PIECES

½	cup (1 stick) butter or margarine, softened
1	cup granulated sugar
2	large eggs
1	teaspoon vanilla extract
2½	cups all-purpose flour
1	teaspoon baking powder
1	teaspoon baking soda
1¾	cups M&M'S® Milk Chocolate Candies, divided
1	cup slivered almonds, toasted*
¼	cup unsweetened cocoa powder
2	tablespoons instant coffee granules

To toast almonds, spread in single layer on baking sheet. Bake at 350°F for 7 to 10 minutes until light golden, stirring occasionally. Remove almonds from pan and cool completely before using.

Preheat oven to 350°F. Lightly grease cookie sheets; set aside.

In large bowl, cream butter and sugar until light and fluffy; beat in eggs and vanilla. In medium bowl, combine flour, baking powder and baking soda; blend into creamed mixture. Dough will be stiff. Stir in 1¼ cups M&M'S® Milk Chocolate Candies and nuts.

Divide dough in half. Add cocoa powder and coffee granules to half of the dough, mixing to blend. On well-floured surface, gently knead doughs together just enough to marble. Divide dough in half and gently roll each half into 12×2-inch log; place on prepared cookie sheets at least 4 inches apart. Press remaining ½ cup M&M'S® Milk Chocolate Candies onto outside of both logs.

Bake 25 minutes. Dough will spread. Cool logs 15 to 20 minutes.

Slice each log into 12 slices; arrange on cookie sheet cut-side down. Bake an additional 10 minutes. (For softer biscotti, omit second baking.) Cool completely. Store in tightly covered container.

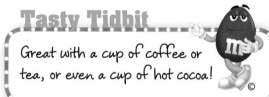

Tasty Tidbit

Great with a cup of coffee or tea, or even a cup of hot cocoa!

Minty Shortbread Squares

MAKES 36 SQUARES

1½	cups (3 sticks) butter, softened
1½	cups powdered sugar
2	teaspoons mint extract, divided
3	cups all-purpose flour
½	cup unsweetened cocoa powder
1¾	cups M&M'S® Milk Chocolate Candies, divided
1	container (16 ounces) white frosting
	Green food coloring (optional)

Preheat oven to 325°F. Lightly grease 15×10×1-inch baking pan; set aside.

In large bowl, cream butter and sugar until light and fluffy; add 1 teaspoon mint extract. In medium bowl, combine flour and cocoa powder; blend into creamed mixture. Stir in 1 cup M&M'S® Milk Chocolate Candies. Dough will be stiff. Press dough into prepared baking pan with lightly floured fingers. Bake 16 to 18 minutes. Cool completely.

Combine frosting, remaining 1 teaspoon mint extract and green food coloring, if desired. Spread frosting over shortbread; sprinkle with remaining ¾ cup M&M'S® Milk Chocolate Candies. Cut into squares. Store in tightly covered container.

Variation: Use 1 (19- to 21-ounce) package fudge brownie mix, prepared according to package directions for chewy brownies, adding 1 teaspoon mint extract to liquid ingredients. Stir in 1 cup M&M'S® Milk Chocolate Candies. Spread dough in lightly greased 13×9×2-inch baking pan. Bake in preheated oven according to package directions. Cool completely. Prepare frosting and decorate as directed above. Store in tightly covered container. Makes 24 squares.

Tasty Tidbit

Chocolate and mint are the perfect companions for these colorful squares.

Chocolate Shortcakes

MAKES 6 SERVINGS

1¼	cups all-purpose flour
½	cup unsweetened cocoa powder
⅔	cup granulated sugar, divided
1	tablespoon baking powder
⅛	teaspoon salt
½	cup (1 stick) cold butter
½	cup milk
1	teaspoon vanilla extract
1¼	cups **M&M'S® MINIS** Milk Chocolate Candies, divided
1	large egg
1	teaspoon water
½	cup cold whipping cream
2	cups sliced strawberries
⅓	cup chocolate syrup

Preheat oven to 425°F.

In medium bowl, combine flour, cocoa powder, ⅓ cup sugar, baking powder and salt. Cut in butter with pastry blender or two knives until mixture resembles coarse crumbs. Add milk and vanilla; mix just until dry ingredients are moistened.

On lightly floured surface, gently knead ¾ cup **M&M'S® MINIS** Milk Chocolate Candies into dough until evenly dispersed. Roll or pat out to ½-inch thickness. Cut with 3-inch round biscuit cutter; place on ungreased cookie sheet. If necessary, reroll scraps of dough in order to make 6 shortcakes. In small bowl, combine egg and water; brush lightly over dough.

Bake 12 to 14 minutes. Cool on cookie sheet 1 minute. Remove to wire racks; cool completely.

In large bowl, beat whipping cream until soft peaks form. Add remaining ⅓ cup sugar; beat until stiff peaks form. Reserve ½ cup whipped cream.

Split shortcakes and place bottom of each on plate; divide strawberries evenly among shortcakes. Top with remaining whipped cream; sprinkle with ¼ cup **M&M'S® MINIS** Milk Chocolate Candies. Replace tops of shortcakes; drizzle with chocolate syrup. Garnish with reserved whipped cream and remaining ¼ cup **M&M'S® MINIS** Milk Chocolate Candies. Serve immediately.

Green's "Dare to Dip 'em" Donuts

MAKES 12 DONUTS AND 12 DONUT HOLES

¼ cup (½ stick) butter, softened

⅓ cup granulated sugar

1 egg

½ teaspoon vanilla extract

1¾ cups all-purpose flour, divided

1 teaspoon baking powder

1 teaspoon ground cinnamon

½ teaspoon baking soda

¼ teaspoon salt

⅓ cup buttermilk

Vegetable oil for frying

2 tablespoons powdered sugar

Chocolate Glaze (recipe follows)

½ cup M&M'S® MINIS Milk Chocolate Candies

In large bowl, cream butter and granulated sugar until light and fluffy; beat in egg and vanilla. In medium bowl, combine flour, baking powder, cinnamon, baking soda and salt. Alternately add one-third flour mixture and half of buttermilk to creamed mixture, ending with flour mixture. Wrap and refrigerate dough 2 to 3 hours.

On lightly floured surface, roll dough to ½-inch thickness. Cut into rings using 2½-inch cookie cutter; reserve donut holes.

Heat about 2 inches oil to 375°F in deep-fat fryer or deep saucepan. Fry donuts, 2 to 3 at a time, about 30 seconds on each side or until

golden brown. Fry donut holes 10 to 15 seconds per side or until golden brown. Remove from oil; drain on paper towels. Cool completely.

Place donut holes and powdered sugar in large plastic food storage bag; seal bag. Shake bag until donut holes are evenly coated. Prepare Chocolate Glaze. Dip donuts into glaze; decorate with M&M'S® MINIS Milk Chocolate Candies. Store in tightly covered container.

Chocolate Glaze

1 cup powdered sugar

1 tablespoon plus 1 teaspoon unsweetened cocoa powder

1 tablespoon plus 1 teaspoon water

¾ teaspoon vanilla extract

In medium bowl, combine powdered sugar and cocoa powder. Stir in water and vanilla; mix well.

Rocky Road Popcorn Balls

MAKES 12 POPCORN BALLS

6	cups unbuttered popped popcorn, lightly salted
2	cups **M&M'S®** Milk Chocolate Candies, divided
1¾	cups peanuts
2	tablespoons butter
4	cups miniature marshmallows

In large bowl, combine popcorn, 1½ cups **M&M'S®** Milk Chocolate Candies and peanuts; set aside. Place remaining ½ cup **M&M'S®** Milk Chocolate Candies in shallow bowl; set aside.

In large saucepan over low heat, combine butter and marshmallows until melted, stirring often. Pour marshmallow mixture over popcorn mixture; stir until well coated.

Form popcorn mixture into 12 balls; roll in **M&M'S®** Milk Chocolate Candies. Store in tightly covered container.

Green's "Easier Than Pie" Pretzel Sticks

MAKES 12 PRETZEL STICKS

1   cup **M&M'S® MINIS** Milk Chocolate Candies

4   squares (1 ounce each) semi-sweet chocolate, divided

12   pretzel rods, divided

4   squares (1 ounce each) white chocolate, divided

Line baking sheet with waxed paper; set aside. Place **M&M'S® MINIS** Milk Chocolate Candies in shallow dish; set aside.

In top of double boiler over hot water, melt 3 squares semi-sweet chocolate. Remove from heat. Dip 6 pretzel rods into chocolate, spooning chocolate to coat about ¾ of each pretzel. Press into and sprinkle with **M&M'S® MINIS** Milk Chocolate Candies; place on prepared baking sheet. Refrigerate until chocolate is firm.

In top of double boiler over hot water, melt 3 squares white chocolate. Remove from heat. Dip remaining 6 pretzel rods into chocolate, spooning chocolate to coat about ¾ of each pretzel. Press into and sprinkle with **M&M'S® MINIS** Milk Chocolate Candies; place on prepared baking sheet. Refrigerate until chocolate is firm.

Place remaining 1 square semi-sweet chocolate in small microwave-safe bowl; place remaining 1 square white chocolate in separate small microwave-safe bowl. Microwave on HIGH 30 seconds; stir. Repeat as necessary until chocolates are completely melted, stirring at 10-second intervals.

Drizzle white chocolate over semi-sweet chocolate-dipped pretzels; drizzle semi-sweet chocolate over white chocolate-dipped pretzels. Sprinkle pretzels with any remaining **M&M'S® MINIS** Milk Chocolate Candies. Refrigerate 10 minutes or until firm. Store tightly covered at room temperature.

Tasty Tidbit

These pretzel sticks are pretty enough to give as a gift. ©

Take-Along Snack Mix

MAKES ABOUT 3½ CUPS

1   tablespoon butter or margarine

2   tablespoons honey

1   cup toasted oat cereal, any flavor

½   cup coarsely broken pecans

½   cup thin pretzel sticks, broken in half

½   cup raisins

1   cup M&M'S® MINIS Milk Chocolate Candies

In large heavy skillet over low heat, melt butter. Add honey; stir until blended. Add cereal, nuts, pretzels and raisins; stir until all pieces are evenly coated. Continue cooking over low heat 10 minutes, stirring frequently. Remove from heat; immediately spread on waxed paper until cool. Add M&M'S® MINIS Milk Chocolate Candies. Store in tightly covered container.

Peanut Butter Crispy Treats

MAKES ABOUT 3 DOZEN TREATS

4   cups toasted rice cereal

1¾   cups M&M'S® MINIS Milk Chocolate Candies

4   cups mini marshmallows

½   cup creamy peanut butter

¼   cup (½ stick) butter or margarine

⅛   teaspoon salt

Combine cereal and M&M'S® MINIS Milk Chocolate Candies in lightly greased baking pan; set aside.

Melt marshmallows, peanut butter, butter and salt in heavy saucepan over low heat, stirring occasionally until mixture is smooth. Pour melted mixture over cereal mixture, tossing lightly until thoroughly coated.

Gently shape into 1½-inch balls with buttered fingers. Place on waxed paper; cool at room temperature until set. Store in tightly covered container.

Variation: After cereal mixture is thoroughly coated, press lightly into greased 13×9×2-inch pan. Cool completely; cut into bars. Makes 24 bars.

Take-Along Snack Mix

Triple Chocolate Parfaits

MAKES 8 SERVINGS

⅔	cup granulated sugar
¼	cup unsweetened cocoa powder
2½	tablespoons cornstarch
2	cups milk
1	large egg
1	tablespoon butter
1	teaspoon vanilla extract
8	slices (½-inch each) packaged chocolate or marbled pound cake
1¼	cups **M&M'S® MINIS** Milk Chocolate Candies, divided
2	cups thawed frozen nondairy whipped topping

In medium saucepan, combine sugar, cocoa powder and cornstarch; stir in milk. Cook over medium heat, stirring often, until mixture comes to a boil. Boil 1 minute, stirring constantly. Remove from heat.

In small bowl, beat egg lightly; stir in ½ cup hot milk mixture. Stir egg mixture into hot milk mixture in saucepan. Cook over medium heat 2 minutes, stirring constantly. Remove from heat; stir in butter and vanilla. Let pudding cool 15 minutes; stirring occasionally.

Just before serving, cut cake into cubes. Divide half of cake cubes among 8 (8-ounce) parfait glasses. Evenly layer half of pudding, ½ cup **M&M'S® MINIS** Milk Chocolate Candies and 1 cup whipped topping. Repeat layers. Decorate with remaining ¼ cup **M&M'S® MINIS** Milk Chocolate Candies. Serve immediately.

Tasty Tidbit

If you're short on time, prepare 2 packages (4-serving size each) instant chocolate pudding instead of making this stove-top version. Then assemble the parfaits as directed.

Tie-Dyed Pie

MAKES 8 SERVINGS

2 packages (4-serving size each) white chocolate instant pudding mix

2½ cups cold milk

½ teaspoon vanilla extract

1½ cups thawed frozen nondairy whipped topping

1¼ cups **M&M'S®** MINIS Milk Chocolate Candies, divided

1 prepared (9-inch) dark chocolate cookie crumb pie crust

Additional nondairy whipped topping for garnish

In large bowl, combine pudding mix and milk; stir until slightly thickened. Add vanilla. Stir in whipped topping and 1 cup M&M'S® MINIS Milk Chocolate Candies. Spread in cookie crumb crust. Freeze 1 hour or until firm.

Let sit 10 minutes at room temperature before serving. Garnish with additional whipped topping and remaining ¼ cup M&M'S® MINIS Milk Chocolate Candies. Store covered in freezer.

Tasty Tidbit

Turn any day into a celebration with this cool and creamy colorful pie.

Gorp Bars

MAKES ABOUT 36 BARS

2½ cups thin pretzel sticks, broken in half

2 cups bite-size crispy corn cereal squares

1½ cups **M&M'S®** Milk Chocolate or Peanut Candies

1 cup banana chips

¾ cup golden raisins

½ cup (1 stick) butter or margarine

⅓ cup creamy peanut butter

1 bag (10-ounces) marshmallows

In large bowl, combine pretzels, cereal, M&M'S® Candies, banana chips and raisins.

In medium saucepan, melt together butter, peanut butter and marshmallows. Stir over low heat until mixture is smooth. Immediately pour over cereal mixture, mixing until all ingredients are thoroughly coated.

Press lightly into greased 13×9-inch pan. Let stand until firm. Cut into 2-inch squares.

Fanciful Party Mix

MAKES ABOUT 5 CUPS

1¾ cups **M&M'S® MINIS** Milk Chocolate Candies

1 cup banana chips, coarsely broken

1 cup honey roasted peanuts

1 cup raisins

Combine all ingredients until well blended. Store in tightly covered container.

Bird's Nest Cookies

MAKES ABOUT 3 DOZEN COOKIES

1⅓ cups (3½ ounces) sweetened shredded coconut

1 cup (2 sticks) butter or margarine, softened

½ cup granulated sugar

1 large egg

½ teaspoon vanilla extract

2 cups all-purpose flour

¾ teaspoon salt

1¾ cups M&M'S® MINIS Milk Chocolate Candies, divided

Preheat oven to 300°F. Spread coconut on ungreased cookie sheet. Toast in oven, stirring until coconut just begins to turn light golden, about 25 minutes. Remove coconut from cookie sheet; set aside. Increase oven temperature to 350°F.

In large bowl, cream butter and sugar until light and fluffy; beat in egg and vanilla. In medium bowl, combine flour and salt; blend into creamed mixture. Stir in 1 cup M&M'S® MINIS Milk Chocolate Candies. Form dough into 1¼-inch balls. Roll heavily in toasted coconut. Place 2 inches apart on lightly greased cookie sheets. Make indentation in center of each cookie with thumb.

Bake 12 to 14 minutes or until coconut is golden brown. Remove cookies to wire racks; immediately fill indentations with remaining M&M'S® MINIS Milk Chocolate Candies, using scant teaspoonful for each cookie. Cool completely.

Ultimate Rocky Road Cups

MAKES 24 CUPS

¾ cup (1½ sticks) butter or margarine

4 squares (1 ounce each) unsweetened baking chocolate

1½ cups granulated sugar

3 large eggs

1 cup all-purpose flour

1¾ cups M&M'S® Milk Chocolate Candies

¾ cup coarsely chopped peanuts

1 cup mini marshmallows

Preheat oven to 350°F. Generously grease 24 (2½-inch) muffin cups or line with paper or foil liners.

Place butter and chocolate in large microwave-safe bowl. Microwave on HIGH 1 minute; stir. Microwave on HIGH an additional 30 seconds; stir until chocolate is completely melted. Add sugar and eggs, one at a time, beating well after each addition; blend in flour.

In separate bowl, combine M&M'S® Milk Chocolate Candies and nuts; stir 1 cup mixture into brownie batter. Divide batter evenly among prepared muffin cups.

Bake 20 minutes. Combine remaining candy mixture with marshmallows; divide evenly among muffin cups, topping hot brownies. Return to oven; bake 5 minutes longer. Cool completely before removing from muffin cups. Store in tightly covered container.

Mini Ultimate Rocky Road Cups:

Prepare recipe as directed using M&M'S® MINIS Milk Chocolate Candies, dividing batter among 60 generously greased 2-inch mini muffin cups. Bake 15 minutes. Sprinkle with topping mixture; bake 5 minutes longer. Cool completely before removing from cups. Store in tightly covered container. Makes about 60 mini cups.

Ultimate Rocky Road Squares:

Prepare recipe as directed, spreading batter into generously greased 13×9×2-inch baking pan. Bake 30 minutes. Sprinkle with topping mixture; bake 5 minutes longer. Cool completely. Cut into squares. Store in tightly covered container. Makes 24 squares.

Delicious Dominos

MAKES 2 DOZEN BROWNIES

6   squares (1 ounce each) semi-sweet chocolate

6   tablespoons butter

2   large eggs

⅓   cup honey

1   teaspoon vanilla extract

½   cup all-purpose flour

½   teaspoon baking powder

    Dash salt

1¼   cups **M&M'S® MINIS** Milk Chocolate Candies, divided

    White Icing (recipe follows)

Preheat oven to 350°F. Line 8×8×2-inch baking pan with aluminum foil, leaving 1½-inch overhang on two sides. Lightly grease foil; set pan aside.

Place chocolate and butter in large microwave-safe bowl. Microwave on HIGH 1 minute; stir. Repeat as necessary until chocolate is completely melted, stirring at 10-second intervals. Let cool slightly. Stir in eggs, honey and vanilla.

In medium bowl, combine flour, baking powder and salt; add to chocolate mixture. Stir in 1 cup **M&M'S® MINIS** Milk Chocolate Candies. Spread mixture in prepared pan.

Bake 20 to 25 minutes or just until center feels springy. Cool completely on wire rack. Lift brownies out of pan using foil. Cut into 2×1¼-inch rectangles.

Prepare White Icing. Spoon icing into small resealable plastic sandwich bag; seal bag. Cut tiny piece off one corner of bag (not more than ⅛ inch). Pipe icing in line across middle of each brownie bar. Decorate with remaining ¼ cup **M&M'S® MINIS** Milk Chocolate Candies to resemble dominos using icing to secure candies to top. Store in tightly covered container.

White Icing: In medium bowl, combine 1 cup powdered sugar, 1 tablespoon warm water and ¼ teaspoon vanilla extract until desired consistency.

Tasty Tidbit

For even easier Delicious Dominos, prepare and bake your favorite brownie mix as the package directs, then decorate as suggested above.

Crispy's Vanishing Pancakes

MAKES 6 TO 8 (5-INCH) PANCAKES

2	cups all-purpose flour
1	tablespoon granulated sugar
1½	teaspoons baking powder
½	teaspoon baking soda
½	teaspoon salt
2	large eggs
1¾	cups buttermilk
¼	cup vegetable oil
¾	cup **M&M'S®** Milk Chocolate Candies, divided
	Butter and maple syrup

Lightly grease and preheat griddle or large skillet over medium heat.

In large bowl, combine flour, sugar, baking powder, baking soda and salt. In medium bowl, beat eggs; gradually add buttermilk and oil until well blended. Blend egg mixture into flour mixture just until moistened.

For each pancake, pour about ½ cup batter onto hot griddle or skillet over medium heat. Sprinkle with about 1 tablespoon **M&M'S®** Milk Chocolate Candies. Cook until tops of pancakes appear dry; turn with spatula and cook 2 minutes or until golden brown.

Serve with butter, maple syrup and remaining ¼ cup **M&M'S®** Milk Chocolate Candies.

Tasty Tidbit

Start your day in a colorful way with these yummy pancakes!

Peanut Butter Mini Muffins

MAKES 3 DOZEN MINI MUFFINS

⅓	cup creamy peanut butter
¼	cup (½ stick) butter, softened
¼	cup granulated sugar
¼	cup firmly packed light brown sugar
1	large egg
¾	cup buttermilk
3	tablespoons vegetable oil
¾	teaspoon vanilla extract
1½	cups all-purpose flour
¾	teaspoon baking powder
½	teaspoon baking soda
½	teaspoon salt
1¼	cups **M&M'S® MINIS** Milk Chocolate Candies, divided
	Chocolate Glaze (recipe follows)

Preheat oven to 350°F. Lightly grease 36 (1¾-inch) mini muffin cups or line with paper or foil liners; set aside.

In large bowl, cream peanut butter, butter and sugars until light and fluffy; beat in egg. Beat in buttermilk, oil and vanilla. In medium bowl, combine flour, baking powder, baking soda and salt; gradually blend into creamed mixture. Divide batter evenly among prepared muffin cups. Sprinkle batter evenly with ¾ cup **M&M'S® MINIS** Milk Chocolate Candies.

Bake 15 to 17 minutes or until toothpick inserted in center comes out clean. Cool completely on wire racks.

Prepare Chocolate Glaze. Place glaze in resealable plastic sandwich bag; seal bag. Cut tiny piece off one corner of bag (not more than ⅛ inch). Drizzle glaze over muffins. Decorate with remaining ½ cup **M&M'S® MINIS** Milk Chocolate Candies; let glaze set. Store in tightly covered container.

Chocolate Glaze: In top of double boiler over hot water, melt 2 (1-ounce) squares semi-sweet chocolate and 1 tablespoon butter. Stir until smooth; let cool slightly.

Whip 'em Up Wacky Waffles

MAKES 4 BELGIAN WAFFLES

1½   **cups biscuit baking mix**
1   **cup buttermilk**
1   **large egg**
1   **tablespoon vegetable oil**
½   **cup M&M'S® MINIS Milk Chocolate Candies, divided**

Powdered sugar and maple syrup

Preheat Belgian waffle iron.

In large bowl, combine baking mix, buttermilk, egg and oil until well mixed.

Spoon about ½ cup batter into hot waffle iron. Sprinkle with about 2 tablespoons M&M'S® MINIS Milk Chocolate Candies; top with about ½ cup batter. Close lid and bake until steaming stops, 1 to 2 minutes.*

Sprinkle with powdered sugar and serve immediately with maple syrup and additional M&M'S® MINIS Milk Chocolate Candies.

*Check the manufacturer's directions for recommended amount of batter and baking time.

Chocolate Waffles: Substitute 1¼ cups biscuit baking mix, ¼ cup unsweetened cocoa powder and ½ cup granulated sugar for biscuit baking mix. Prepare and cook as directed above.

Tasty Tidbit

These waffles make a great dessert too! Serve them with a scoop of ice cream, chocolate sauce and a sprinkle of M&M'S® MINIS Milk Chocolate Candies.

Crispy's Irresistible Peanut Butter Marbles

MAKES 5 DOZEN COOKIES

1   package (18 ounces) refrigerated peanut butter cookie dough

2   cups M&M'S® MINIS Milk Chocolate Candies, divided

1   cup crisp rice cereal, divided (optional)

1   package (18 ounces) refrigerated sugar cookie dough

¼   cup unsweetened cocoa powder

In large bowl, combine peanut butter dough, 1 cup M&M'S® MINIS Milk Chocolate Candies and ½ cup cereal, if desired. Remove dough to small bowl; set aside.

In large bowl, combine sugar dough and cocoa powder until well blended. Stir in remaining 1 cup M&M'S® MINIS Milk Chocolate Candies and remaining ½ cup cereal, if desired. Remove half the dough to small bowl; set aside.

Combine half the peanut butter dough with half the chocolate dough by folding together just enough to marble. Shape marbled dough into 8×2-inch log. Wrap log in plastic wrap. Repeat with remaining doughs. Refrigerate logs 2 hours.

To bake, preheat oven to 350°F. Cut dough into ¼-inch-thick slices. Place about 2 inches apart on ungreased cookie sheets. Bake 12 to 14 minutes. Cool 1 minute on cookie sheets; cool completely on wire racks. Store in tightly covered container.

Pumpkin Surprise Muffins

MAKES 12 MUFFINS

3	ounces cream cheese, softened
2	tablespoons firmly packed light brown sugar
1	cup shredded bran cereal
¾	cup buttermilk
1¼	cups all-purpose flour
¾	cup granulated sugar
1	teaspoon baking powder
1	teaspoon baking soda
1	teaspoon ground cinnamon, divided
¼	teaspoon salt
¼	teaspoon ground ginger
⅛	teaspoon ground nutmeg
½	cup solid pack pumpkin
¼	cup vegetable oil
¼	cup (½ stick) butter, melted
1	large egg
1¼	cups M&M'S® Milk Chocolate Candies, divided
1	cup cream cheese frosting

Preheat oven to 400°F. Lightly grease 12 (2¾-inch) muffin cups or line with paper or foil liners; set aside.

In small bowl, combine cream cheese and brown sugar; set aside. In medium bowl, combine cereal and buttermilk; let stand 20 minutes. In large bowl, combine flour, granulated sugar, baking powder, baking soda, cinnamon, salt, ginger and nutmeg.

Add pumpkin, oil, butter and egg to cereal mixture; blend well. Stir pumpkin mixture into flour mixture just until all ingredients are moistened. Stir in 1 cup **M&M'S®** Milk Chocolate Candies. Fill each prepared muffin cup ½ full with batter. Spoon 1 teaspoon cream cheese mixture into center of batter in each cup; top with 1 tablespoon remaining batter.

Bake 15 to 18 minutes or until toothpick inserted in center comes out clean. Cool completely on wire racks.

Frost muffins with cream cheese frosting; decorate with remaining ¼ cup **M&M'S®** Milk Chocolate Candies. Store in tightly covered container.

M&M'S® Jam Sandwiches

MAKES 1 DOZEN SANDWICH COOKIES

½ cup (1 stick) butter, softened
¾ cup granulated sugar
1 large egg
1 teaspoon almond extract
½ teaspoon vanilla extract
1⅓ cups all-purpose flour
¼ teaspoon baking powder
¼ teaspoon salt
  Powdered sugar
½ cup seedless raspberry jam
½ cup **M&M'S® MINIS** Milk Chocolate Candies

In large bowl, cream butter and sugar until light and fluffy; beat in egg, almond extract and vanilla. In small bowl, combine flour, baking powder and salt; blend into creamed mixture. Wrap and refrigerate dough 2 to 3 hours.

Preheat oven to 375°F. Working with half the dough at a time on lightly floured surface, roll to ⅛-inch thickness. Cut into desired shapes using 3-inch cookie cutters. Cut out equal numbers of each shape. (If dough becomes too soft, refrigerate several minutes before continuing.) Cut 1½- to 2-inch centers out of half the cookies of each shape. Reroll trimmings and cut out more cookies. Using rigid spatula, carefully transfer shapes to ungreased cookie sheets.

Bake 7 to 9 minutes. Cool on cookie sheets 1 to 2 minutes; cool completely on wire racks.

Sprinkle powdered sugar on cookies with holes. Spread about 1 teaspoon jam on flat side of whole cookies, spreading almost to edges. Place cookies with holes, flat side down, over jam. Place **M&M'S® MINIS** Milk Chocolate Candies over jam in holes. Store between layers of waxed paper in tightly covered container.

M&M'S® Gift Jar Cookie Mix

MAKES 4 DOZEN COOKIES

- ¾   **cup all-purpose flour**
- 1   **teaspoon baking soda**
- ½   **teaspoon salt**
- ½   **teaspoon ground cinnamon**
- ½   **cup chopped walnuts**
- 1   **cup M&M'S® MINIS Milk Chocolate Candies, divided**
- ½   **cup raisins**
- ¾   **cup firmly packed light brown sugar**
- 1¼   **cups uncooked quick oats**

In medium bowl, combine flour, baking soda, salt and cinnamon.

In 1-quart clear glass jar with tight-fitting resealable lid, layer flour mixture, walnuts, ½ cup **M&M'S® MINIS** Milk Chocolate Candies, raisins, brown sugar, remaining ½ cup **M&M'S® MINIS** Milk Chocolate Candies and oats. Seal jar; wrap decoratively.

Give as a gift with the following instructions: Preheat oven to 350°F. Lightly grease cookie sheets; set aside. In large bowl, beat ¾ cup (1½ sticks) butter, 1 large egg and ¾ teaspoon vanilla extract until well blended. Stir in contents of jar until well blended. Roll into 1-inch balls and place about 2 inches apart on prepared cookie sheets. Bake 12 to 15 minutes. Cool 2 minutes on cookie sheets; cool completely on wire racks. Store in tightly covered container.

Frozen Treats

Color-Bright Ice Cream Sandwiches

MAKES ABOUT 24 ICE CREAM SANDWICHES

¾	cup (1½ sticks) butter or margarine, softened
¾	cup creamy peanut butter
1¼	cups firmly packed light brown sugar
1	large egg
1	teaspoon vanilla extract
1½	cups all-purpose flour
1	teaspoon baking soda
¼	teaspoon salt
1¾	cups M&M'S® Milk Chocolate Candies, divided
2	quarts vanilla or chocolate ice cream, slightly softened

Preheat oven to 350°F.

In large bowl, cream butter, peanut butter and brown sugar until light and fluffy; beat in egg and vanilla. In medium bowl, combine flour, baking soda and salt; blend into creamed mixture. Stir in 1⅓ cups **M&M'S®** Milk Chocolate Candies. Shape dough into 1¼-inch balls. Place about 2 inches apart on ungreased cookie sheets. Gently flatten to about ½-inch thickness with fingertips. Place 7 or 8 of the remaining **M&M'S®** Milk Chocolate Candies on each cookie; press in lightly.

Bake 10 to 12 minutes or until edges are light brown. Do not overbake. Cool about 1 minute on cookie sheets; cool completely on wire racks.

Assemble cookies in pairs with about ⅓ cup ice cream; press cookies together lightly. Wrap each sandwich in plastic wrap; freeze until firm.

Blue's Chillin' Banana Coolers

MAKES 4 SERVINGS

2 ripe medium bananas, peeled

4 flat wooden ice cream sticks

½ cup **M&M'S® MINIS** Milk Chocolate Candies

⅓ cup hot fudge ice cream topping, at room temperature

Line baking sheet with waxed paper; set aside. Cut each banana in half crosswise. Insert wooden stick about 1½ inches into center of cut end of each banana. Place on prepared baking sheet; freeze until firm, at least 2 hours.

Place M&M'S® MINIS Milk Chocolate Candies in shallow dish. Place fudge sauce in separate shallow dish. Working with 1 banana at a time, place frozen banana in fudge sauce; turn banana and spread fudge sauce evenly onto banana with small rubber scraper. Immediately place banana on plate with M&M'S® MINIS Milk Chocolate Candies; turn to coat lightly. Return to baking sheet in freezer. Repeat with remaining bananas.

Freeze until fudge sauce is very firm, at least 2 hours. Let stand 5 minutes before serving. Store tightly covered in freezer.

Tasty Tidbit

These tasty banana coolers are the perfect snack for a warm summer day.

Brownie Sundae Cake

MAKES 12 SLICES

1   package (19 to 21 ounces) fudge brownie mix, prepared according to package directions for cake-like brownies

1   cup **M&M'S®** Milk Chocolate Candies

½   cup chopped nuts (optional)

1   quart vanilla ice cream, softened

¼   cup caramel or butterscotch ice cream topping

Line 2 (9-inch) round cake pans with aluminum foil, extending slightly over edges of pans. Lightly spray bottoms with vegetable cooking spray; set aside.

Preheat oven as brownie mix package directs. Divide brownie batter evenly between pans; sprinkle ½ cup **M&M'S®** Milk Chocolate Candies and ¼ cup nuts, if desired, over each pan. Bake 23 to 25 minutes or until edges begin to pull away from sides of pan. Cool completely. Remove layers by lifting foil from pans.

To assemble cake, reline the sides and bottom of one 9-inch springform pan with plastic wrap, place one brownie layer, topping-side down, in 9-inch springform pan. Carefully spread ice cream over brownie layer; drizzle with ice cream topping. Place second brownie layer on top of ice cream layer, topping-side up; press down lightly. Wrap in plastic wrap and freeze until firm. Remove from freezer about 15 minutes before serving. Remove side of pan. Cut into wedges.

Tasty Tidbit

An ice cream and brownie lover's delight!

Clown-Around Cones

MAKES 4 SERVINGS

4 waffle cones

½ cup **M&M'S® MINIS** Milk Chocolate Candies, divided

Prepared decorator icing

½ cup hot fudge ice cream topping, divided

4 cups any flavor ice cream, softened

1 (1.5- to 2-ounce) chocolate candy bar, chopped

¼ cup caramel ice cream topping

Decorate cones as desired with **M&M'S® MINIS** Milk Chocolate Candies, using decorator icing to attach; let set.

For each cone, place 1 tablespoon hot fudge topping in bottom of cone. Sprinkle with 1 teaspoon **M&M'S® MINIS** Milk Chocolate Candies. Layer with ¼ cup ice cream; sprinkle with ¼ of candy bar. Layer with ¼ cup ice cream; sprinkle with 1 teaspoon **M&M'S® MINIS** Milk Chocolate Candies. Top with 1 tablespoon caramel topping and remaining ½ cup ice cream. Wrap in plastic wrap and freeze until ready to serve.

Just before serving, top each ice cream cone with 1 tablespoon hot fudge topping; sprinkle with remaining **M&M'S® MINIS** Milk Chocolate Candies. Serve immediately.

Tasty Tidbit

This decadent frozen treat brings out the kid in all of us!

Banana Split Cups

MAKES 3 DOZEN COOKIES

1   **package (18 ounces) refrigerated chocolate chip cookie dough**

⅔   **cup M&M'S® MINIS Milk Chocolate Candies, divided**

1   **ripe medium banana, cut into 18 slices and halved**

¾   **cup chocolate syrup, divided**

2¼   **cups any flavor ice cream, softened**

     Aerosol whipped topping

¼   **cup chopped maraschino cherries**

Lightly grease 36 (1¾-inch) mini muffin cups. Cut dough into 36 equal pieces; roll into balls. Place 1 ball in bottom of each muffin cup. Press dough onto bottoms and up sides of muffin cups; chill 15 minutes. Press ⅓ cup M&M'S® MINIS Milk Chocolate Candies into bottoms and sides of dough cups.

Preheat oven to 350°F. Bake cookies 8 to 9 minutes. Cookies will be puffy. Remove from oven; gently press down center of each cookie. Return to oven 1 minute. Cool cookies in muffin cups 5 minutes. Remove to wire racks; cool completely.

Place 1 banana half slice in each cookie cup; top with ½ teaspoon chocolate syrup. Place about ½ teaspoon M&M'S® MINIS Milk Chocolate Candies in each cookie cup; top with 1 tablespoon ice cream. Top each cookie cup with ½ teaspoon chocolate syrup, whipped topping, remaining M&M'S® MINIS Milk Chocolate Candies and 1 maraschino cherry piece. Store covered in freezer.

Tasty Tidbit

Bite-sized banana splits are just right for little (and big) tummies!

"Make Your Own Sundae" Pie

MAKES 8 SERVINGS

1	cup hot fudge ice cream topping, warmed and divided
1	prepared (9-inch) vanilla cookie crumb pie crust
6	cups vanilla ice cream, softened
1	cup caramel ice cream topping, warmed and divided
¼	cup marshmallow creme
1	tablespoon milk
⅔	cup **M&M'S® MINIS** Milk Chocolate Candies
¼	cup chopped nuts
	Aerosol whipped topping and maraschino cherry for garnish

Spread ½ cup hot fudge topping on bottom of crust; freeze 10 minutes. Spread 1 cup ice cream over fudge layer; freeze 10 minutes. Spread ½ cup caramel topping over ice cream layer; freeze 10 minutes. Mound scoops of ice cream over caramel layer. Cover and freeze until ready to serve.

Just before serving, in small bowl combine marshmallow creme and milk. Microwave on HIGH 10 seconds; stir until well combined. Drizzle pie with remaining ½ cup hot fudge topping, remaining ½ cup caramel topping and marshmallow sauce. Sprinkle with ⅓ cup **M&M'S® MINIS** Milk Chocolate Candies and nuts. Garnish with whipped topping, remaining ⅓ cup **M&M'S® MINIS** Milk Chocolate Candies and maraschino cherry. Serve immediately.

M&M'S® Brain Freezer Shake

MAKES 2 (1¼-CUP) SERVINGS

2   cups any flavor ice cream

1   cup milk

¾   cup **M&M'S® MINIS** Milk Chocolate Candies, divided

     Aerosol whipped topping

     Additional M&M'S® MINIS Milk Chocolate Candies for garnish

In blender container, combine ice cream and milk; blend until smooth. Add ½ cup M&M'S® MINIS Milk Chocolate Candies; blend just until mixed. Pour into 2 glasses.

Top each glass with whipped topping; sprinkle with remaining ¼ cup M&M'S® MINIS Milk Chocolate Candies. Serve immediately.

"Here's Looking at You" Yummies

MAKES 2 DOZEN TREATS

½   **cup creamy or crunchy peanut butter**

2   **tablespoons butter, softened**

¾   **to 1 cup powdered sugar, divided**

1¼   **cups crisp rice cereal**

1¼   **cups M&M'S® MINIS Milk Chocolate Candies, divided**

4   **squares (2 ounces each) white almond bark**

     Red decorating gel

Line cookie sheet with waxed paper; set aside.

In large bowl, combine peanut butter and butter. Stir in ½ cup powdered sugar until well blended. Stir in cereal and 1 cup M&M'S® MINIS Milk Chocolate Candies. Stir in ¼ cup powdered sugar. If mixture is too sticky, stir in remaining ¼ cup powdered sugar. Shape dough into 1½-inch balls. Place on prepared cookie sheet. Refrigerate 1 hour.

Line another cookie sheet with waxed paper; set aside. Melt almond bark according to package directions. Dip one ball into almond bark; gently shake off excess. Place treat on prepared cookie sheet. Decorate with remaining ¼ cup M&M'S® MINIS Milk Chocolate Candies and decorating gel to look like eyes. Store in tightly covered container.

Festive Holiday Rugelach

MAKES ABOUT 6 DOZEN COOKIES

1½   **cups (3 sticks) butter or margarine, softened**

12   **ounces cream cheese, softened**

3½   **cups all-purpose flour, divided**

½   **cup powdered sugar**

¾   **cup granulated sugar, divided**

1½   **teaspoons ground cinnamon**

1¾   **cups M&M'S® MINIS Milk Chocolate Candies, divided**

     Powdered sugar

Preheat oven to 350°F. Lightly grease cookie sheets; set aside.

In large bowl, cream butter and cream cheese. Slowly work in 3 cups flour. Divide dough into 6 equal pieces and shape into squares. Lightly flour dough, wrap in waxed paper and refrigerate at least 1 hour.

Combine remaining ½ cup flour and ½ cup powdered sugar. Remove one piece of dough at a time from refrigerator; roll out on surface dusted with flour-sugar mixture to 18×5×⅛-inch-thick strip. Combine granulated sugar and cinnamon. Sprinkle dough strip with 2 tablespoons cinnamon-sugar mixture. Sprinkle about ¼ cup **M&M'S® MINIS** Milk Chocolate Candies on wide end of each strip. Roll dough starting at wide end to completely enclose baking bits. Cut strip

into 1½-inch lengths; place seam side down about 2 inches apart on prepared cookie sheets. Repeat with remaining ingredients.

Bake 16 to 18 minutes or until golden. Cool completely on wire racks. Sprinkle with powdered sugar. Store in tightly covered container.

Variation: For crescent shapes, roll each piece of dough into 12-inch circle. Sprinkle with cinnamon-sugar mixture. Cut into 12 wedges. Place about ½ teaspoon **M&M'S® MINIS** Milk Chocolate Candies at wide end of each wedge and roll up to enclose baking bits. Place seam side down on prepared cookie sheets and proceed as directed.

Tasty Tidbit

you'll love this colorful rendition of a traditional recipe!

Giant Easter Egg Cookies

MAKES ABOUT 2½ DOZEN COOKIES

2	cups (4 sticks) butter or margarine, softened
½	cup granulated sugar
½	cup firmly packed light brown sugar
1	large egg
1	teaspoon vanilla extract
3½	cups all-purpose flour
½	teaspoon salt
1	cup chopped pecans
1¾	cups **M&M'S®** Milk Chocolate Candies, divided
	Decorating icing

Preheat oven to 375°F.

In large bowl, cream butter and sugars until light and fluffy; beat in egg and vanilla. In medium bowl, combine flour and salt; blend into creamed mixture. Stir in nuts and 1¼ cups **M&M's®** Milk Chocolate Candies. Drop by ¼ cupfuls about 4 inches apart onto lightly greased cookie sheets; flatten each into egg shape about 4×2¾ inches.

Bake 11 to 13 minutes or until lightly browned. Carefully remove to wire racks to cool completely. Decorate with icing and remaining ½ cup **M&M's®** Milk Chocolate Candies. Store in tightly covered container.

Tasty Tidbit

Add these "eggs" to any basket for a special spring treat!

Ornament Cupcakes

MAKES 16 CUPCAKES

1   cup all-purpose flour

2   teaspoons baking powder

¼   teaspoon salt

½   cup granulated sugar

¼   cup firmly packed light brown sugar

¼   cup (½ stick) butter, softened

½   cup orange juice

½   teaspoon grated orange peel

½   teaspoon vanilla extract

2   large eggs

1   cup M&M'S® MINIS Milk Chocolate Candies, divided

1   cup white frosting

     Assorted food colorings

     Red or black licorice whips, cut into 3-inch lengths

8   gumdrops, cut in half lengthwise

Preheat oven to 350°F. Lightly grease 16 (2¾-inch) muffin cups or line with paper or foil liners; set aside.

In large bowl, combine flour, baking powder and salt; stir in sugars. Beat in butter, orange juice, orange peel and vanilla. Beat 2 minutes. Add eggs; beat 2 minutes. Divide batter evenly among prepared muffin cups. Sprinkle evenly with ½ cup M&M'S® MINIS Milk Chocolate Candies.

Bake 20 minutes or until toothpick inserted in center comes out clean. Cool completely on wire racks.

In small bowl, combine frosting and desired food coloring. Spread frosting over cupcakes. For each ornament hanger, insert both ends of licorice piece into gumdrop half; place on cupcakes. Decorate with remaining ½ cup M&M'S® MINIS Milk Chocolate Candies.

Tasty Tidbit

Serve these festive cupcakes at this year's tree-trimming party.

Haunted House

MAKES 1 CENTERPIECE

1	cup (2 sticks) butter, softened
2	cups firmly packed light brown sugar
¾	cup light corn syrup
2	large eggs
5¼	cups all-purpose flour
2	teaspoons baking soda
2	teaspoons ground ginger
1	teaspoon ground allspice
½	teaspoon ground cinnamon
	Royal Icing (recipe follows)
	Decorating Glaze (recipe follows)
	Assorted food colorings
2	cups M&M'S® MINIS Milk Chocolate Candies

In large bowl, cream butter and brown sugar until light and fluffy; beat in corn syrup and eggs. In medium bowl, combine flour, baking soda and spices; blend into creamed mixture. Wrap and refrigerate dough 2 to 3 hours.

Preheat oven to 350°F. Lightly grease cookie sheets; set aside.

Working with one-third of dough at a time on lightly floured surface, roll to ⅛-inch thickness. Cut out 2 (10×6-inch) rectangles for roof and 2 shapes for each side of the house; place on prepared cookie sheets. Roll scraps to ⅛-inch thickness and cut out with Halloween cookie cutters; place 2 inches apart on prepared cookie sheets. Bake 5 to 7 minutes or until lightly browned at edges. Let cool 2 minutes on cookie sheets; cool completely on wire rack.

Cover 12-inch square piece of heavy cardboard with aluminum foil to use as base for house. Prepare Royal Icing. Spoon icing into small resealable plastic sandwich bag; seal bag. Cut tiny piece off one corner of bag. Pipe icing on edges of all house pieces including bottom; "glue" house together at seams and onto base. Let stand at least 1 hour or until icing is set, supporting walls with heavy drinking glass.

Prepare Decorating Glaze; tint with food colorings as desired. Spread house and cookies with glaze and decorate with M&M'S® MINIS Milk Chocolate Candies.

Royal Icing: In large bowl, beat 3 egg whites at high speed of electric mixer until foamy. Gradually add 3 cups powdered sugar; beat at low speed until moistened. Increase mixer speed to high and beat until stiff.

Decorating Glaze: In large bowl, combine 4 cups powdered sugar and ¼ cup water until smooth. If necessary, add additional water, 1 teaspoon at a time, to make a medium-thick pourable glaze.

Haunted Idea: "Glue" decorated Halloween cookies onto the house with Royal Icing. Use extra cookies to create an outdoor scene around the house.

Edible Easter Baskets

MAKES 3 DOZEN COOKIES

1   package (about 18 ounces) refrigerated sugar cookie dough

1   cup M&M'S® MINIS Milk Chocolate Candies, divided

1   teaspoon water

1   to 2 drops green food coloring

¾   cup sweetened shredded coconut

¾   cup any flavor frosting

     Red licorice whips, cut into 3-inch lengths

Lightly grease 36 (1¾-inch) mini muffin cups.

Cut dough into 36 equal pieces; roll into balls. Place 1 ball in each muffin cup. Press dough onto bottom and up sides of each muffin cup; chill 15 minutes. Press ⅓ cup M&M'S® MINIS Milk Chocolate Candies into bottoms and sides of dough cups.

Preheat oven to 350°F. Bake cookies 8 to 9 minutes. Cookies will be puffy. Remove from oven; gently press down center of each cookie. Return to oven 1 minute. Cool cookies in muffin cups 5 minutes. Remove to wire racks; cool completely.

In medium bowl, combine water and food coloring. Add coconut; stir until evenly tinted. In each cookie cup, layer 1 teaspoon frosting, 1 teaspoon tinted coconut and 1 teaspoon M&M'S® MINIS Milk Chocolate Candies. Push both licorice ends into frosting to make basket handle. Store in tightly covered container.

MINI'S Messy Mix

MAKES ABOUT 8 CUPS SNACK MIX

5 cups unbuttered popped popcorn, lightly salted

1 cup pretzel nuggets

½ cup slivered almonds, toasted and lightly salted

¼ cup (½ stick) butter

¼ cup light corn syrup

¾ cup firmly packed light brown sugar

⅓ cup red cinnamon candies

1 cup **M&M'S® MINIS** Milk Chocolate Candies

1 cup plain or cinnamon animal crackers

½ cup sweetened dried cranberries

Preheat oven to 250°F. Divide popcorn evenly between two large bowls. To each bowl add half the pretzel nuggets and half the almonds; set aside. Lightly grease 2 large baking pans; set aside.

In medium saucepan over low heat, combine butter and corn syrup until melted; stir in brown sugar. Cook, stirring constantly, until sugar is melted and mixture comes to a boil. Boil mixture 5 minutes, stirring often. With lightly greased spatula, stir half of sugar mixture into one bowl of popcorn mixture until evenly coated. Add cinnamon candies

to remaining sugar mixture in saucepan. Cook, stirring constantly, until candies are melted. Stir cinnamon-sugar mixture into remaining popcorn mixture until evenly coated. Spread each portion popcorn mixture in even layer in separate prepared pans.

Bake 1 hour, stirring every 15 minutes with lightly greased spoon to separate popcorn. Cool completely in pans on wire racks.

In large bowl, combine both popcorn mixtures, M&M'S® MINIS Milk Chocolate Candies, animal crackers and cranberries. Store in tightly covered container.

Tasty Tidbit

Kids go wild for this outrageous snack mix!

Mini Pizza Cookies

MAKES 8 COOKIES

1   package (about 18 ounces) refrigerated sugar cookie dough

2   cups (16 ounces) prepared pink frosting

M&M'S® Milk Chocolate Candies

Variety of additional toppings such as shredded sweetened coconut, granola, raisins, nuts, small pretzels, snack mixes, sunflower seeds, popcorn and mini marshmallows

Preheat oven to 350°F. Lightly grease cookie sheets; set aside.

Divide dough into 8 equal portions. On lightly floured surface, roll each portion of dough into ¼-inch-thick circle; place circles about 2 inches apart on prepared cookie sheets.

Bake 10 to 13 minutes or until golden brown on edges. Cool completely on wire racks. Spread top of each pizza with frosting; sprinkle with **M&M'S®** Milk Chocolate Candies and 2 or 3 suggested toppings.

Colorful S'mores Squares

MAKES 24 SQUARES

½   cup (1 stick) butter or margarine, softened

1   cup granulated sugar

3   large eggs

1   teaspoon vanilla extract

2   cups graham cracker crumbs

1¾   cups **M&M'S®** MINIS Milk Chocolate Candies, divided

1   cup marshmallow creme

Preheat oven to 350°F. Lightly grease 13✕9✕2-inch pan.

In large bowl, cream butter and sugar until light and fluffy; beat in eggs and vanilla. Stir in graham cracker crumbs until well blended. Stir in 1 cup **M&M'S®** MINIS Milk Chocolate Candies. Spread batter into prepared pan; bake 30 minutes.

Dollop marshmallow creme over hot crust; spread gently and evenly over crust. Sprinkle with remaining ¾ cup **M&M'S®** MINIS Milk Chocolate Candies; bake 5 minutes. Cool completely. Cut into squares.

Mini Pizza Cookies

Easy Decorating

Colorful Caramel Apples

MAKES 6 APPLES

1	package (14 ounces) caramels, unwrapped
2	tablespoons water
6	wooden craft sticks
6	medium apples, rinsed and completely dried
1	cup chopped nuts, divided
1	cup **M&M'S® MINIS** Milk Chocolate Candies, divided
2	squares (1 ounce each) semi-sweet chocolate
2	squares (1 ounce each) white chocolate

Line baking sheet with waxed paper; set aside. In medium saucepan over medium heat, combine caramels and water; cook, stirring constantly, until melted. Remove from heat.

Insert 1 craft stick into stem end of each apple. Dip apples, one at a time, into caramel mixture, coating completely. Remove excess caramel mixture by scraping apple bottom across rim of saucepan. Place on waxed paper.

Place ½ cup nuts in shallow dish; set aside. Place ½ cup **M&M'S® MINIS** Milk Chocolate Candies in separate shallow dish; set aside. Place semi-sweet chocolate in small microwave-safe bowl. Microwave on HIGH 1 minute; stir. Repeat as necessary until chocolate is completely melted, stirring at 10-second intervals. Drizzle chocolate over 3 apples. Roll apples in nuts and **M&M'S® MINIS** Milk Chocolate Candies. Refrigerate apples until firm.

Place white chocolate in small microwave-safe bowl. Microwave on HIGH 1 minute; stir. Repeat as necessary until white chocolate is completely melted, stirring at 10-second intervals. Drizzle white chocolate over remaining 3 apples. Roll apples in remaining nuts and **M&M'S® MINIS** Milk Chocolate Candies. Refrigerate until firm.

Ladybug Cupcakes

MAKES 24 LADYBUGS

1 package (18.25 ounces) any flavor cake mix, plus ingredients to prepare cupcakes

1 container (16 ounces) vanilla frosting

Red food coloring

⅔ cup dark chocolate frosting

M&M'S® Chocolate Candies; malted milk balls, cut in half; chocolate candy wafers

12 black licorice laces, cut into 48 pieces

Prepare cupcakes according to directions on package. Line 24 (2¾-inch) muffin cups with paper liners. Fill each cup with ⅔ cup batter.

Bake according to directions on package; remove from oven. While waiting for cupcakes to completely cool, tint vanilla frosting with red food coloring.

Once cooled, frost tops of cupcakes with red frosting. Spoon dark chocolate frosting into a resealable bag. Snip a small corner from the bag. Pipe a line of dark chocolate frosting down the center of each cupcake. Decorate with M&M'S® Chocolate Candies, malted milk balls or chocolate wafers for face, eyes and spots, and licorice for antennae.

Tasty Tidbit

These are the sweetest little cupcake creatures!

Go Fish

MAKES 2½ DOZEN COOKIES

½   cup (1 stick) butter, softened
¾   cup granulated sugar
¼   cup firmly packed light brown
      sugar
1   large egg
1   large egg white
½   teaspoon vanilla extract
2   cups all-purpose flour
1¼ teaspoons ground cinnamon
1   teaspoon baking powder
1   cup white frosting
      Assorted food colorings
1   cup M&M'S® MINIS Milk
      Chocolate Candies

In large bowl, cream butter and sugars until light and fluffy; beat in egg, egg white and vanilla. In medium bowl, combine flour, cinnamon and baking powder; add to creamed mixture. Wrap and refrigerate dough 2 to 3 hours.

Preheat oven to 325°F. Working with half the dough at a time on lightly floured surface, roll to ¼-inch thickness. Cut into fish shapes using 3-inch cookie cutters. Place about 2 inches apart on ungreased cookie sheets. Bake 10 to 12 minutes. Cool 2 minutes on cookie sheets; cool completely on wire racks.

Tint frosting desired colors. Frost cookies and decorate with **M&M'S® MINIS** Milk Chocolate Candies. Store in tightly covered container.

Tasty Tidbit
Going fishing has never been this much fun.

Beautiful Butterflies

MAKES 2 DOZEN COOKIES

1 package (about 18 ounces) refrigerated sugar cookie dough

24 wooden craft sticks

1 container (16 ounces) white frosting

Assorted food colorings

1 cup **M&M'S® MINIS** Milk Chocolate Candies

Preheat oven to 325°F.

Working with half the dough at a time on lightly floured surface, roll to ¼-inch thickness. Cut into butterfly shapes using 3-inch cookie cutters. Press on craft sticks and place about 2 inches apart on ungreased cookie sheets. Bake 10 to 12 minutes. Cool 2 minutes on cookie sheets; cool completely on wire racks.

Divide frosting among separate bowls; tint with food colorings as desired. Spread colored frosting over cookies; decorate with **M&M'S® MINIS** Milk Chocolate Candies. Let set. Store in tightly covered container.

Tasty Tidbit

This butterfly basket will brighten up anyone's day.

3-D Holiday Cookies

MAKES 18 (3-D) COOKIES

½	cup (1 stick) butter, softened
⅓	cup granulated sugar
2	tablespoons firmly packed light brown sugar
1	large egg
½	teaspoon vanilla extract
1½	cups all-purpose flour
½	teaspoon baking powder
⅛	teaspoon salt
	Decorating Glaze (recipe follows)
	Assorted food colorings
½	cup **M&M'S®** MINIS Milk Chocolate Candies

In large bowl, cream butter and sugars until light and fluffy; beat in egg and vanilla. In small bowl, combine flour, baking powder and salt; blend into creamed mixture. Wrap and refrigerate dough 2 to 3 hours.

Preheat oven to 375°F. Working with half of dough at a time on lightly floured surface, roll to ⅛-inch thickness. Cut into pairs of desired shapes using 3-inch cookie cutters. Re-roll trimmings and cut out more pairs. Place cutouts 1 inch apart on ungreased cookie sheets.

Bake 5 to 7 minutes. Immediately cut 1 cookie of each pair in half vertically. Cool on cookie sheets 1 minute; cool completely on wire racks.

Prepare Decorating Glaze. Tint glaze with food colorings as desired. Spread line of glaze down cut edge of half cookie. Press half cookie to middle of whole cookie; let set. Repeat with remaining half cookie, attaching half cookie to middle back of whole cookie. Spread glaze over entire 3-D cookies; let set. Using glaze to attach, decorate cookies with **M&M'S®** MINIS Milk Chocolate Candies. Store in tightly covered container.

Decorating Glaze: In large bowl, combine 4 cups powdered sugar and ¼ cup water until smooth. If necessary, add additional water, 1 teaspoon at a time, to make a medium-thick pourable glaze.

Tasty Tidbit

Decorating these cookies is only half the fun!

Light Up the Sky Cake

MAKES 16 TO 20 SERVINGS

1   package (18.25 ounces) any flavor cake mix, plus ingredients to prepare mix

¼   cup (½ stick) butter, softened

2½   cups powdered sugar, divided

2   to 3 tablespoons milk

¼   teaspoon vanilla extract

     Blue food coloring

1½   cups M&M'S® MINIS Milk Chocolate Candies

Prepare and bake cake as directed on package for 13×9-inch cake. Cool cake completely on wire rack.

In large bowl, cream butter until light. Add 1¼ cups powdered sugar; beat until fluffy. Blend in milk and vanilla. Beat in remaining 1¼ cups powdered sugar until frosting is smooth. Add enough food coloring to make frosting dark blue.

Frost cake and decorate with M&M'S® MINIS Milk Chocolate Candies to look like exploding fireworks.

Loony Lollies

MAKES 4 LOLLIPOPS

½	cup powdered sugar
1	tablespoon milk
4	giant flat lollipops
½	cup **M&M'S® MINIS** Milk Chocolate Candies

In small bowl, combine powdered sugar and milk until smooth. Place icing in resealable plastic sandwich bag; seal bag. Cut tiny piece off one corner of bag (not more than ⅛ inch). Decorate lollipops with **M&M'S® MINIS** Milk Chocolate Candies, using icing to attach. Let set 10 to 15 minutes. Store in tightly covered container.

Dino-Mite Dinosaurs

MAKES 2 DOZEN COOKIES

1	cup (2 sticks) butter, softened
1¼	cups granulated sugar
1	large egg
2	squares (1 ounce each) semi-sweet chocolate, melted
½	teaspoon vanilla extract
2⅓	cups all-purpose flour
1	teaspoon baking powder
¼	teaspoon salt
1	cup white frosting
	Assorted food colorings
1	cup M&M'S® MINIS Milk Chocolate Candies

In large bowl, cream butter and sugar until light and fluffy; beat in egg, chocolate and vanilla. In medium bowl, combine flour, baking powder and salt; add to creamed mixture. Wrap and refrigerate dough 2 to 3 hours.

Preheat oven to 350°F. Working with half the dough at a time on lightly floured surface, roll to ¼-inch thickness. Cut into dinosaur shapes using 4-inch cookie cutters. Place about 2 inches apart on ungreased cookie sheets. Bake 10 to 12 minutes. Cool 2 minutes on cookie sheets; cool completely on wire racks.

Tint frosting to desired colors. Frost cookies and decorate with **M&M'S® MINIS** Milk Chocolate Candies. Store in tightly covered container.

Green's Lucky Cake

MAKES 16 TO 20 SERVINGS

1 package (18.25 ounces) any flavor cake mix, plus ingredients to prepare mix

½ teaspoon water

2 to 3 drops green food coloring

½ cup sweetened shredded coconut

6 tablespoons butter, softened

3¾ cups powdered sugar, divided

3 to 4 tablespoons milk

½ teaspoon vanilla extract

Blue food coloring

1 cup M&M'S® MINIS Milk Chocolate Candies

Prepare and bake cake as directed on package for 13×9-inch cake. Cool cake completely on wire rack.

In small bowl, combine water and food coloring. Add coconut and stir until evenly tinted; set aside. In large bowl, cream butter until light. Add 2 cups powdered sugar; beat until fluffy. Blend in 3 tablespoons milk and vanilla. Beat in remaining 1¾ cups powdered sugar until frosting is smooth. Add additional milk, 1 teaspoon at a time, if necessary to make frosting spreadable. Tint frosting desired shade of blue.

Frost cake and decorate with tinted coconut and M&M'S® MINIS Milk Chocolate Candies.

Index

METRIC CONVERSION CHART

VOLUME MEASUREMENTS (dry)

$^{1}/_{8}$ teaspoon = 0.5 mL
$^{1}/_{4}$ teaspoon = 1 mL
$^{1}/_{2}$ teaspoon = 2 mL
$^{3}/_{4}$ teaspoon = 4 mL
1 teaspoon = 5 mL
1 tablespoon = 15 mL
2 tablespoons = 30 mL
$^{1}/_{4}$ cup = 60 mL
$^{1}/_{3}$ cup = 75 mL
$^{1}/_{2}$ cup = 125 mL
$^{2}/_{3}$ cup = 150 mL
$^{3}/_{4}$ cup = 175 mL
1 cup = 250 mL
2 cups = 1 pint = 500 mL
3 cups = 750 mL
4 cups = 1 quart = 1 L

VOLUME MEASUREMENTS (fluid)

1 fluid ounce (2 tablespoons) = 30 mL
4 fluid ounces ($^{1}/_{2}$ cup) = 125 mL
8 fluid ounces (1 cup) = 250 mL
12 fluid ounces (1$^{1}/_{2}$ cups) = 375 mL
16 fluid ounces (2 cups) = 500 mL

WEIGHTS (mass)

$^{1}/_{2}$ ounce = 15 g
1 ounce = 30 g
3 ounces = 90 g
4 ounces = 120 g
8 ounces = 225 g
10 ounces = 285 g
12 ounces = 360 g
16 ounces = 1 pound = 450 g

DIMENSIONS

$^{1}/_{16}$ inch = 2 mm
$^{1}/_{8}$ inch = 3 mm
$^{1}/_{4}$ inch = 6 mm
$^{1}/_{2}$ inch = 1.5 cm
$^{3}/_{4}$ inch = 2 cm
1 inch = 2.5 cm

OVEN TEMPERATURES

250°F = 120°C
275°F = 140°C
300°F = 150°C
325°F = 160°C
350°F = 180°C
375°F = 190°C
400°F = 200°C
425°F = 220°C
450°F = 230°C

BAKING PAN SIZES

Utensil	Size in Inches/Quarts	Metric Volume	Size in Centimeters
Baking or Cake Pan (square or rectangular)	8×8×2	2 L	20×20×5
	9×9×2	2.5 L	23×23×5
	12×8×2	3 L	30×20×5
	13×9×2	3.5 L	33×23×5
Loaf Pan	8×4×3	1.5 L	20×10×7
	9×5×3	2 L	23×13×7
Round Layer Cake Pan	8×1½	1.2 L	20×4
	9×1½	1.5 L	23×4
Pie Plate	8×1¼	750 mL	20×3
	9×1¼	1 L	23×3
Baking Dish or Casserole	1 quart	1 L	—
	1½ quarts	1.5 L	—
	2 quarts	2 L	—